PITCHING SALES!

A COMPLETE GUIDE TO BECOMING A SALES PROFESSIONAL

Outwork, Outperform, and Outsell

BRYAN CHARLEAU

Pitching Sales! A complete Guide to Becoming a Sales Professional

Printed in Canada

ISBN 978-1-7386516-0-3 (Paperback)
ISBN 978-1-7386516-2-7 (Ebook)
ISBN 978-1-7386516-1-0 (Audiobook)

Book cover and interior design: Najdan Mancic

Special Thank you to:

Michael Shrider, David Rothenberger, Abigail Wise, Najdan Mancic, Dana, and My Family and Friends for their contributions to this book and unconditional support

CONTENTS

PART I

OBJECTIVE OF THIS BOOK

NOT YOUR TYPICAL SALES BOOK

SALES GURUS, MULTI-MILLIONAIRES, OVERNIGHT SUCCESS stories, million-dollar sales techniques, "get rich quick" methods—these are the types of high-net-worth individuals and topics you are used to seeing in sales books. Well, not this book. Not yet anyways. That might not be the opening line you were expecting but, if I am being honest, I am no different than you career wise. I have not built my capital to a point where I have financial freedom nor am I on the backside of my career where I feel I have learned all I need to know. I am still waking up every morning, continuously working towards my personal and professional goals, struggling, and succeeding in the business world within the depths of the sales profession. I remind myself on a daily basis that sales is a constantly evolving career that needs to be practiced and honed on an infinite loop.

With this in mind, you may be asking what someone like myself is able to offer you. I don't blame you, that is a fair question. Although we may have many similarities, if you are new to sales, there is one thing that separates us. I have grinded for over a decade gaining sales experience, carving out my own path through my personal hardships along with the guidance of others who have been through the same thing. I have found success across different industries throughout my career, consistently finishing at or near the top in sales every year regardless of what company I was at. There is no perfect formula to mastering sales as every route will be personalized through experience and mentorship. However, there are wrong turns and pitfalls that can be avoided by new professionals that only someone with experience can tell you about. This book is designed to prevent you from getting caught in these weeds and allow you to navigate through the turbulent situations you are bound to encounter.

I have structured the book in hopes of providing a comfort level for you. I have not glorified my current situation in an attempt to manipulate you into believing you can achieve similar success simply by reading this book. I feel those professionals are disconnected from the everyday struggles that new salespeople come upon in the field. Throughout this book, I will be tackling scenarios you will face in the near future or may have even already come across. I hope to establish a connection with you to help understand the pains that I went through getting my career started. I want you to know that I learned the hard way, much like many others in the sales profession.

Rather than telling you what to do, I aim to offer insight into how you can connect the dots much faster than I did, allowing you to perpetuate the highs and soften the lows and allowing you to recognize that at the beginning, you do not need to navigate sales on your own. It is extremely beneficial to learn the preliminary skills in the profession with a figurative cheat sheet to expedite your growth. This book is a conglomeration of my own experience along with the guidance of my mentors and successful colleagues that I have had the honour to meet and work with along the way.

OBJECTIVE OF THIS BOOK

What I want you to realize is that this book is not meant to provide you with sales theory, lines to overcome objections, or the formula to a "get rich quick potion". It's meant for my younger self that walked into that boiler room atmosphere, for the young professional just finishing school looking to define themselves, for the struggling student trying to find a job to pay their tuition, for the individual who has heard about the opportunities of commissioned income, and for those looking to master the basic principles of sales to accelerate your career trajectory. Yes, this book is meant for anyone who has been led to the sales profession but doesn't know where to start or who to turn to. It doesn't matter if you've been in sales for a long time and need to relearn the basics to realign bad habits, if you're the individual who has just accepted their first sales job, or if you're a person who has yet to apply and wants to learn about what it will take to succeed. My goal is for this information to connect with you on a level that makes it understandable, logical, and, most importantly, **actionable**. The concepts are not designed to overwhelm you, but their importance cannot be overstated and will stay with you for your entire career. Ultimately, there will be ups and downs in both life and career. When you're in a funk, I want you to be able to pull this book out and remember where you started and how to get yourself back on track. I want this to not only be your first sales book, but one you can re-read for a lifetime.

Like every sales professional, I had to pursue this career the hard way which, according to the workforce, is "the only way". When I struggled out of the gate, I assumed it was standard to take some time to get acquainted to the profession. This was not uncommon, and I did not feel much pressure at the beginning. I spoke with colleagues and learned from those around me while still keeping in mind that advice given at the entry level can range in content and ethics depending on the individual.

Over time, I began to feel more comfortable but recognized that I was a long way from any true monetary gains or personal confidence with what I was doing. After a few months with no sales, I began consulting outside sources for information. I purchased as many books as I could and began to dive in. (I have a full list of book recommendations in a later section if you are interested). The more books that I read trying to improve myself, the more that I realized I was in over my head—I wasn't ready for these theories and closing techniques. I wasn't ready to implement these ideas as I wasn't even at the stage where I had prospective buyers interested in the product. I was not only trying to run before I could walk. No, I was attempting to sprint before I could walk.

Everywhere I looked, I found books that were full of FANTASTIC information from well-respected authors within the sales profession, but I could not find anything to help me get started. I was unable to find anything to get my feet on the ground and understand the profession at the fundamental level. These authors were helping readers get from good to great. What I needed was the recipe to take raw talent and enthusiasm and mold it into someone that could create some momentum early and excel long-term. As good as the information was in these books, it was useless until I hacked my way through the thick brush that presents itself to every entry level salesperson.

In the end, myself and thousands of other sales professionals have made it to the other side, but it doesn't have to be this difficult. My objective is to give you a few cheat codes to soar past those trying to figure it out on their own. For each topic in this book, I asked myself "Would this have helped me when I started?" If the answer was "Yes", then I included it. Some topics may seem basic, but trust me, if it's in here, that means it was important enough to reiterate and expand upon.

Now that you understand WHY I wrote this book, I want to finalize my objectives by outlining WHAT I want you to take away from this book. I want to help prepare you for the beginning stages of your career and I want to help guide you through some of the unexpected situations you may find yourself in. I want you to understand that I spoke to highly successful friends and colleagues while developing the ideas within this book so that I could receive a full range of perspective from different industries, ages, and experiences. I wanted this book to reflect not only the views and opinions of what I have faced, but what others have endured on their own journey to success. I truly believe this is an easy-to-read book, filled with important and often overlooked information brought to you from my own personal experiences as well as other firsthand accounts from high level individuals. If followed, this guidance will propel you and your career in the right direction.

WHERE I STARTED

"You're crazy" were the first words out of my mothers' mouth when I told her I had accepted a job that offered 100% commission in an industry that I had NO IDEA about. When I say NO IDEA, I mean it. When I spoke to my future manager in the beginning stages of my interview process, he asked me about my sales experience and my knowledge of the industry. It was clear to him he wouldn't be hiring me based on the latter. However, he was intrigued by a few key things. Firstly, the amount of time I had spent learning about sales theory and putting that theory into practice within several different industry sectors. Secondly, being comfortable with a fully commissioned job in an industry I had no experience in. Later, he would tell me it was gut instinct that ultimately led him to hire me; whatever it was, he was willing to take a chance on me.

From my perspective, accepting the job was an easy decision—I was willing to bet on myself. I have done this my whole life in school, sports, and career. When you bet on yourself, you're able to take accountability for your own success or failures. I knew that I was willing to put the effort into learning the industry and that my sales experience would eventually overlap, leading to success. I was looking at the long-term outcome even though I knew there were going to be short-term pains and that money would be scarce to start.

Money scarcity was something I had already grown accustomed to being a long-time student and only working entry level jobs out of school. Also, it doesn't hurt to have extra motivation, as I didn't want to eat ramen noodles my whole life, even though they don't hurt in a pinch. I didn't get into business to play it safe; I decided against earning a conservative wage to live a conservative life. I entered this profession to excel and earn an income that I couldn't attain playing it safe. I did it to pursue a life I could only imagine; knowing I earned it by working hard and dedicating myself to my craft.

Growing up, I never thought I would be in sales. I was not the son of anyone in the sales profession, my father was a police officer for thirty-nine years and my mother was a correctional officer for thirty-seven years before they retired. As you can image, my brother and I didn't get away with much as kids. I spent my childhood playing every sport possible, eventually leading to a university football career. I spent my summers earning money by working at a variety of local farms. I spent five years on a tobacco farm, one summer on a sod farm, and then another on a cherry farm. Obviously, none of these directly related to my sales career, but a lot of characteristics developed from these experiences transferred into my DNA. Hard work, perseverance, dedication, and finishing what you start. All facets of life that can only be learned through experiences.

My sales career started in what can only be described as the oddest location possible. It wasn't at an office building, a training facility, or even at a tradeshow. Nope, it started at a gas station. I was selling car wax to people as they stood at their vehicle pumping gas. Talk about being thrown into the fire. I was spending eight hours a day in the middle of summer perched at a gas station approaching people to demonstrate how magnificent this car wax was. As one might expect, this was a little easier said than done. I had about five minutes to introduce myself, explain the product, establish enough trust to demonstrate it, show it off, and close the sale before they paid and left. Talk about an accelerated sales cycle. The other wrinkle to add, this was also a fully commissioned job (Not the same as the one stated above). At about $5 a can, there was no being shy, or you were not going home with much jingle in your pocket.

The turnover rate was unbelievable, as I found myself teaching new employees almost daily. Somehow, I made it through the entire summer and ended up making enough in commission to help pay for my schooling. I learned a lot of excellent lessons that summer, the most important of which was that sales can be a rewarding job. However, it takes a lot of effort, a lot of rejection, and some thick skin, all of which we will touch on later in this book. *I would love to know about some of your first sales jobs. If you can beat the conditions of this*

one and still want to stay in sales, I applaud your gumption.
#myfirstsalesjob

From there, I ended up taking small sales jobs here and there throughout my university life, sharpening my skills and paying bills, but I was not certain it would be my future career choice. I was focusing on education in the classroom and football on the field. When the dust finally settled, I finished with a bachelor's degree in human relations and a minor in business and marketing. Upon graduation, the universe brought me back to sales when I came across a company that sold sports hospitality packages to major corporations around North America. I wasn't seeking a sales job at the time, but knowing that I had previous success, I wasn't opposed to it. The added bonus being that if I sold the sports packages, I got to go to the events and meet the clients in person. Sounds too good to be true, right? **It was.**

I won't name the company, but as a bright-eyed and bushy tailed university graduate, this seemed like a great way to start off my career with a combination of business, sports marketing, and sales. It began with a nice three-day, fully paid training session with lots of excellent material. I was very pleased with the amount of time they spent training new recruits as the position didn't require any sales experience. However, on my first day at the office, I came crashing back to reality. It was a literal boiler room scene that I was not prepared for (An excellent movie to watch, but a sales environment to avoid). There were no walls or cubicles, it was an open room with joining desks divided into sections based on what you were selling. My sports section had eight desks in two rows joined face to face, with a manager at each end. There I was, staring at the person across from me, friends I had made within my training class beside me, my bosses at either end, and mayhem going on behind me. To be honest, I didn't know what to expect, but it wasn't this.

We didn't even have computers at our desk, we had our phone and a holder for pens and paper. There were two old computers in the corner that we were able to reserve on limited use to research new leads. My boss would keep a strict limit on usage, as we were to do our prospecting "after hours". I was handed a very long-winded pitch that was riddled with typos and grammatical errors. I was to practice the "pitch" with the people around me until I felt comfortable enough to start cold calling corporations.

This company kept files from all their previous leads in its database, so I was given these old leads to practice on. I quickly came to find out that these leads had been called dozens of times by old reps and many were not happy to hear from me. I heard the line "I told the last rep from your company to take me off the list, I will never buy from you!" Hey, at least I was getting people on the phone! This was better than the co-workers dialing specific numbers they knew would go right to voicemail just to get their call rates up.

As things progressed, I was told to call 100+ million-dollar companies and attempt to talk to their CEO/President to pitch them on our events. Easy enough, right? As the realization of the job really set in, I began to grasp exactly what the hell I had gotten myself into. It was horrible. The company would track how many outgoing calls you had made and how many minutes you spent on the phone each day. The next morning, the boss would then announce to the sales team, as a group, how each person performed. It was like calling up Apple with number provided on the website and asking for Tim Cook. I know that may seem like hyperbole, but that's actually what they were asking us to do! As time went on, I promised myself that I would not be staying in this job forever, but that I would learn as much as I could while I was there. I wasn't going to leave until I got myself a sale so that I could see the sweet reward of a well-earned commission cheque.

I ended up leaving after ten months making a grand total of two sales. From the outside, it may seem like I didn't give it a lot of time, but the average new employee would last for about two weeks before realizing the cruelty of the job and vanish. I even witnessed a new hire leave for lunch on her first day and not return. She lasted three hours! I felt like a seasoned veteran by the time I moved on. In my ten months, I saw a lot, I learned a lot about the profession, and I learned a lot about myself. The biggest realization that I took from this job was the various personalities that you come across in a sales environment. I came to understand that you don't have to like every style of selling or even agree with it. You are, however, doing yourself a disservice not learning from each one. All of them have their strengths and weaknesses and understanding this will help you to mold your own style as you move forward and continually evolve as a professional. With this mindset, the job became the best and worst situation of my life, all at the same time.

After I left that job, I took some time off but eventually continued in the industry at a competitor for the next eight months. Ultimately, I decided that this was not the lifestyle that I was looking for. I hated the 9-5 grind, sitting in the office making cold calls with no direction in my career. I had another brief stop at a tech company selling software systems, which was met with more success. However, the pay was lousy, the commissions were few and far between, and there was no career growth.

I finally waved the white flag. I left the city, the profession, and I did not expect to return. Two years later, the fully commissioned opportunity I referred to earlier presented itself, which brings us to where we are today. Even though this is just a brief insight into some of my past jobs, you can see that it was not glamourous, it was not quick, and it certainly was not easy. Fast forward to my current situation and I have now been with my company for six years. Nothing has been handed to me or come easy, but success is presenting itself in ways I could never have foreseen.

There have been some very difficult days, especially in the beginning. I was learning a new industry, readjusting to a fully commissioned paycheque, adapting to outside sales, building a home office, and re-establishing my sales goals. I can, with 100% certainty, assure you that I would not have been hired by this company if it wasn't for my previous sales training and experience. Even if I had been hired by them, I would not have had ANY success in this job. Heck, I might have even left by lunch on my first day. The entire reason I was able to grow a career in an unknown industry with unfamiliar working conditions was because I had built a rock solid and unbreakable foundation of sales habits from my previous jobs and training. I didn't learn these skills the easy way or take any shortcuts. I gutted it out, walking into an office that I dreaded every morning, and continued to push myself to make sales and better myself even though I thought it to be an unattainable task at the time.

I continually thank my former self for waking up early and pulling myself out of bed because without those lessons learned, I would not have been presented with this amazing opportunity. Survival was a powerful motivator and in those early days, I was just scraping by. I had to adjust and learn on the fly just to make sure the bills were paid. At the time, I was not aware that I was forming these integral work habits, but in times like that it can be difficult to see the forest when you're staring at the tree in front of you. Since those initial days, I have been able to grow my professional career while writing this book. The hope being that it will help you build your own rock-solid foundation to reach your career goals faster than I was able to. I promise that if you follow and implement the basics outlined in this book, you will expedite your learning curve and hardwire habits that you will continue to use for the rest of your sales career.

SUMMARY BEFORE WE BEGIN

As we move along, you will learn more about me both personally and professionally. This is to help you understand the trials and tribulations that I have gone through, and how I have been able to accept mistakes. I have evolved, found success, and continue to grow my career in hopes of achieving my professional goal of financial freedom and personal self-fulfillment. Obviously, everybody's career will take a different path, and you will encounter situations that are different than mine and others around you. Soon enough you will notice several similarities that overlap throughout the profession regardless of the industry you're in. The more you're able to adapt to this, the more successful the beginning of your career can be. I want you to be able to pinpoint potential shortcomings based on your inexperience, while also providing solutions for you to quickly overcome these situations.

Instead of a standard chapter-based book, I have divided it into different sections each covering a wide range of topics. As previously stated, every reader will be coming into this book with different goals and life experiences, so I wanted to start right from the beginning. I show you the basics on how to properly apply for a sales job, what fears you need to overcome, positive habits you need to develop, implementing a long-term motivational mindset, goal setting, and much more. I want to be clear, concise, and talk to you as a fellow salesperson who understands exactly what you're going through.

PART II

IS SALES RIGHT FOR ME?

WHAT TO EXPECT IN THE SALES PROFESSION

THIS MIGHT SEEM LIKE A loaded statement right off the hop, but if you are interested in sales, it is an important aspect to consider. This profession is scattered with every type of individual you can imagine. There are people from all walks of life with differing personality traits; some find success while others fall short.

Ultimately, success in sales can be measured in a number of different perspectives. Some will attribute it to monetary earnings, positions of power, tenure, or a combination of these. Others find pride in growing a company from the ground up, helping customers fulfil a need, and providing exceptional service. Success will ultimately lie in the eye of the beholder, but you do not need to have all the answers to this early in your career. At this point, you are a blank slate and a clean canvas. This is not meant to scare anyone off; in fact, it is quite the opposite. Regardless of whether you think you're too shy, lack confidence, or any preconceived notion that you feel will limit you in the profession. You need to realize there have been people who have had these same thoughts, who have overcome them, and who have become extremely successful. This book is designed to help you identify your own strengths and weaknesses, giving you guidance to reinforce the positives and reassess the weaker points.

In this profession, there are many outside stereotypes with regards to salespeople. The brash, pushy, money-hungry jerks or the smooth talking, manipulative individuals trying to sell you snake oil or a clunky car. While these people do exist, you will realize that this profession is filled with genuine, good people. All of them are trying to provide for themselves and their families while dealing with the ups and downs, just like everyone else. Don't feel like you have to become someone else to find success; being yourself is the best place to build from. This only strengthens the idea that all individuals have a place in sales, creating a balanced yin and yang within the profession.

On top of dealing with colleagues that have a range of personalities, you're going to run into different type of managers and bosses as well. Some will be qualified, and some won't. Some will understand the delicate nature of dealing with a new hire, and some won't. You cannot assume that because they're in a position of authority and have had success that they are equipped to deal with your particular situation or have a managerial style that intertwines with your personality. Understand that no matter how friendly, open, and honest you are, you will run into fellow employees, bosses, and executives that you just do not mesh with. This can be said for any profession, but things are definitely magnified in sales when you need to account for quota, commission, and internal competition. These dynamics can bring out the worst in people, especially if you are all vying for the same prospects within the office.

Unfortunately, this can be the culture created within some companies. It is important to not lose sight of your own morals and to deal with each situation on a case-by-case basis to decide if this is the best environment for you. True professionals understand that the better person you are and become, the better salesperson you will be. In the big picture, sales will take years of effort, training, evolving, and practice to become a master. However, at the root of it all, the very foundation of every successful salesperson starts with **integrity**. Someone who is willing to put a customer's needs first, one who is willing to help his fellow employee without any expectation of a repayment, and one who is willing to take others under their wing to show them the proverbial ropes. Obviously, there will be people who do not possess these qualities and will find some success, but I am a firm believer that integrity is the single most important trait to have on the path to success in sales.

The next factor to consider when entering the profession is what type of sales environment you're starting in and what it is you're striving for. Unless you have a very strong network or an inside connection, you're going to have to cut your teeth at an entry level position in sales. You're going to begin as a small fish in a big pond. There is nothing wrong with this, as it is a great place to start, and it will open your eyes to the profession. This is where almost all high-end sales professionals started. Whether you are with a large corporation or a small business, it is always important to have long and short-term career goals. I understand it is much more difficult to map out a success plan when you are just beginning. With this in mind, it is important to be realistic early on with multiple short-term goals focused on learning and achieving small successes. This can then be followed by optimistic long-term goals and an idea of where you want to be down the road.

These will not only help you balance out expectations, but it will keep you pushing forward when you run into roadblocks and frustrations in the short-term. These goals can be fluid and change as your situation progresses, but they are always important to have. They will vary greatly between individuals based on their own life situations and the industries they are working within. The more you grow into your job, the more specific your goals can become and the more you can leverage what you have learned to reach them. As an example, I have listed one of my first long-term goals below.

When I started in the profession, I knew that I wanted to be in outside sales; I wanted to be negotiating in boardrooms, visiting high-end clients in their offices, and supplying a product that helped change customers' businesses for the better. Being face-to-face with a customer while having a sales conversation changes the entire dynamic of the situation. It allows you to build rapport and better understand the needs and wants of the customer by including non-verbal communication to the sales process. However, there are so many rudimentary things that need to be developed and understood before experiencing this scenario. To truly learn the craft of sales, steady improvement is key. This progression involves some small victories, but also many failures and lessons learned.

HOW TO PREPARE FOR YOUR FIRST SALES JOB

Like any job, preparation is extremely important when looking into a future employer. I challenge you not to be too particular in finding the perfect company within the perfect industry for your first sales job. If you happen to come across an ideal fit, then obviously I recommend attempting to secure this job. For most, however, this scenario will not happen. Be open-minded and look for job openings across many different industries. Preliminary research will be needed; you should read the job description, brush-up on the company, and gain a general understanding of what their expectations of you will be. If it passes the "eye test", then tailor a resume and apply for the position. There will be further research needed later but getting a response and interview is the first step.

Building a Good Resume and Cover Letter

A proper resume is extremely important when applying for any sales job. There are hundreds of different ways they can be designed and laid out. It is hard to know exactly what a prospective employer is looking for when they see yours, but there are definitely some specifics that need to be highlighted.

Keep in mind, your resume will not be given a lot of "eye time" before it is either passed on or put in the maybe pile. I put it this way: a good resume will never get you a job, but a bad one will ensure you don't get hired. A professional one that is well written, properly laid out, and grammatically correct will give you the best opportunity to reach the next step.

I am not going to give advice on how to write your resume, but I am going to suggest that you seek out help from multiple sources to review your final product and to make the changes deemed necessary. It can be helpful to ask someone to candidly review your resume and see if they would bring you in for an interview if it were to come across their desk. There are plenty of websites online to help you with this; make sure you review multiple templates and look for the reoccurring key points that are consistent across the different sources and be sure to include them. If you're still having trouble, there are companies that will design an entire resume for you after a few consultations to learn about your experience and skills.

While on the topic of resumes, it is fascinating to hear how often people do not include cover letters with them. A proper cover letter is the first step for you to separate yourself from the field; it presents the opportunity to showcase your personality and comprehension of the position you are applying for. Keep in mind, you are selling yourself to your prospective employer. A good cover letter shows work ethic, attention to detail, and the willingness to put in extra effort for what you want. When you tailor a cover letter to the specific job that you are applying for, it shows your prospective employer that you did not send out a generic copy to a mass number of job openings.

It shows that you are a serious candidate, and this will greatly improve your chances of landing an interview.

I suggest creating a general cover letter highlighting your assets, and then making specific changes to your main copy for each application depending on the job description. Again, there are a number of ways to lay-out a well-written cover letter. I suggest that you look at online sources and cross-reference the important details that are common among them. If possible, always be sure to specify the individual whom the cover letter is being addressed to. This is a small detail that will automatically put you much further ahead of others who have made a generic opening such as "To Whom it May Concern" or "Dear Sir or Madam".

The final step of this three-step process is presenting your resume and cover letter. Emailing the company with your attached resume followed by a short message outlining the position you are applying for, has become the most common way to apply for a job. In some circumstances, this will be the only method that you can use to get your information into the hands of the right person. However, the most impactful way to make a lasting first impression is to walk into the office of the company you are applying for, and to present a hard copy of your resume and cover letter directly to the one in charge of the hiring process. To properly do this, it may take a little of bit of research on your end to find out who this individual is. This can usually be found on the job listing or the company's website. You may also have to call the office and ask who is responsible for the hiring of the position you are applying for and their usual office hours. The key thing to remember here is that you are applying for a sales job, and that they are looking for an individual who will think outside the box and be bold; someone who is willing to go the extra mile to speak with a decision maker. Every sales job I have ever had has started with me showing up at the office and physically handing in my resume to the person doing the hiring. On one particular occasion, I was granted an interview on the spot. Showing that initiative is a powerful tool in a business world that is becoming increasingly difficult to separate yourself from the pack.

Getting Ready for an Interview

If you are able to secure the interview, it is now time to dig deeper into the company. Study what they sell, the services they provide, who their target market is, how long they have been in business, who the CEO/owner/president is, their mission statement, number of offices they have and where they are located. Read reviews from former employees, reviews from customers (good and bad), how the company has been doing for the last year, the last 3 years, the last 5 years. The internet is an amazing tool and you should be able to find most, if not all of this information in a short period of time.

The bulk of this research should be done after you schedule an interview with the company because you do not want to misuse your time analyzing every detail before you've secured a follow-up. Spending large amounts of time finding the perfect company and the perfect situation before you have even applied could create disappointment and cause you to be discouraged if you do not hear back from them. This research is meant to better prepare you for the interview and to help you avoid joining a "shady" or immoral company that does not have a proper code of business ethics. Ensure that you do not jump to conclusions based on one source, but if you see reoccurring red flags it may be a situation you want to avoid.

All of this preparation and effort have led to the ever-important interview. This is a nerve-wracking and stressful time for most people, but just know that there is no magic formula to nailing an interview. There are many variables based on the industry, the company, and the interviewer. There are, however, a few key factors that can give you an advantage.

Remember, you're applying for a sales position, and you need to be prepared with the research you did on the company and the industry it is situated in. If the interviewer asks questions related to their products, their target market, their industry, or their competitors, being ready with an educated and appropriate response displays a lot of desirable skills. Learning these research skills early will also help to better prepare yourself for sales meetings, presentations, and first contact with prospective customers down the road. You are not at that stage yet but realize that this is a great learning opportunity. The more you know about the company, the industry, and your position the less an interviewer has to explain these details, and the more they can learn about you and the qualities you can bring to the company. Without this preparation, you'll already be playing catch-up with other candidates.

After you thank the interviewer for their time and the opportunity, be sure to ask them when you should expect to hear back. Ensure there is a basic timeline set and that the interview does not end on unclear terms. If you have not heard from them in the timeline that was set, it is up to you to reach out so they can provide you with an update. I will continue to stress this—**you are applying to be a salesperson**—the interviewer wants to see this type of effort and tenacity from an applicant. They may be waiting for a follow-up call or using this as a deciding factor between you and another candidate. Don't wait for the job, go get it! I understand this is not a book on how to get a sales job, but you'll soon appreciate that attention to detail when applying for a job has many transferable skills to the actual job itself. Your ultimate goal is to separate yourself from other applicants in order to earn a position within the company. The same way you earn a sale by separating yourself from the competition by showing why your product or service is more valuable to the end user.

A final, often overlooked aspect for any sales job, is understanding HOW you're going to be compensated. As much as I love sales, there's a reason we're all in it, and that's to make some money. To do this, we need to know what the payment structure is within the company. This is not always as straightforward as it may seem, and if you're new to the profession, this is NOT to be asked during the first interview. Most likely, this will be explained to you by the interviewer. If not, that's okay; there will be plenty of time to ask and understand the structure before you accept the job.

As you gain experience within the profession and you find yourself applying and interviewing for higher level jobs, you will begin to have more leverage in this process, and this may become an acceptable point of discussion. Regardless of when the information is presented to you, it is important to fully comprehend and understand the payment structure. Payment structure can be designed in a variety of different ways with the basics being: Base salary, base salary + bonus(es), base salary + commission, or full commission. There are three standard ways that commissions are calculated as shown in the chart below.

Standard Commission Payout Structures:

TYPE OF COMMISSION	DESCRIPTION	EXAMPLE AT 10% COMMISSION	COMMISSION PAID
Gross Revenue	Percentage based on final price before tax	Unit sold at $1000	$100 ($1000 x 0.1)
Gross Margin	Percentage based on final price before tax, minus cost of good	Unit sold at $1000/ Cost of unit $700	$30 ($300 x 0.1)
Set Amount	Set amount of commission for each item sold, regardless of price	Unit sold at $1000	Pre-determined amount

When looked at on a grander scale, there is no right or wrong way for commissions to be structured; the value lies in understanding it. Some like the security of a base salary and lower commission payment per sale while others prefer a more aggressive commission structure and want to bet on themselves to learn and grow quickly, in order to achieve higher overall earnings as long as sales numbers are met. The main reason you want to fully comprehend the commission structure is to have a complete understanding of how much income you can realistically make in that position.

The reason I felt it was important to not only include but also emphasize this section is because some companies try to confuse new sales representatives with their payment structure, especially those who have never earned commission before. They advertise with slogans like "Unlimited earning potential with commissions". This allows them to dance around what your true earning potential will be, especially early on. I was a victim to this at one of my first jobs, where they offered below minimum wage, but advertised the potential of unlimited earnings with the commissions. After my first sale, I discovered that I was only making commissions on 70% of the sale because of service fees to the company even though the margins had already been worked into the total price. Looking back, I should have seen the red flags when they dressed up the contract to make it as confusing as possible, and when I didn't fully understand how they were presenting it, I was too intimidated to ask the right questions and have them break down the contract agreement in detail for me. I hope this section helps you better understand the different payment options that may be presented to you. Don't be afraid to reach out to somebody within the profession if do not fully understand what is being offered to you in your new job.

Lastly, on this topic, it is important to understand that when you're earning an income that is commission based, there are different tax implications. If you are new to sales, you are most likely accustomed to your taxes being automatically deducted from your pay, and then submitting your forms at tax time. Often, but not always, your commissions will not be subject to taxes when you receive them. As great as it may seem initially, this money is not free. Eventually, the tax man will come knocking on the door and you will have to report these earnings. While it can be helpful to speak with other employees or the manager about how they normally deal with taxes when it comes to their commission, my best advice would be to ask an accountant or tax professional. Keep in mind, your situation will differ based on where you file your taxes. Most importantly, do not spend this money, before you know these tax implications, or you may be left empty handed when the government ask for it back. Did I learn this the hard way? You bet.

WHY SALES CAN BE THE BEST CAREER CHOICE

I feel that by this point of the book, it should be quite clear that I am passionate about my career choice. I have fully immersed myself into becoming better at my craft and will continue to do so for the rest of my life. Obviously, when you read the title of this section, I am excluding some of the most sought-after career paths that some of us strive for: professional athlete, rock star, or actor in Hollywood. However, when it comes to the more realistic professions, I do not think there are many others that I would choose over sales. Maybe astronaut? Many of the reasons for this will be touched on throughout this book, but I want to bring it to the forefront to give it the attention it deserves.

What is these reasons? Expansion. Growth. Advancement. However, you want to word it, in sales you have the freedom to continually become better, improve your abilities, and you are rarely bound by restrictions. There are very few professions in this world where your real-time income has a direct correlation to the amount of work and effort you're exerting in the moment. In some careers, you can go back to school (which can take years) to specialize in a field, or you can take training programs to expand your knowledge which can lead to promotions and raises. That is all well and good, but in sales, one book, one podcast, one seminar can impact your income the very next day. Becoming more confident in a particular buying situation or learning how to sell a feature of your product can get you a raise on the next call. With this mindset, you can dedicate yourself to your profession and develop habits in order to bring you profits that you never thought possible. Financial freedom is typically a long-term goal for most sales professionals and the best part is, it's attainable! It may take years of discipline, focus, and a commitment to succeed, but you can achieve this goal.

Another major benefit to the sales profession is that it allows you freedom of time. It should be noted that this is very dependent on your industry and current position. I understand that most of the readers of this book will be younger, either in school or just graduating and this will not apply to you in most entry level sales positions. However, this was something I always aspired for. I did not enjoy slugging myself to the office early in the morning using public transit and clocking in by 8am. I did not enjoy having to request days off or relying on ten vacation days per year. I wanted to be able to travel WHILE I worked. I wanted to have control of my own schedule; this would allow me to spend time with my family when I wanted to, not when my manager approved it. Granted, these types of privileges do not come easy, and they may take time to attain. You must constantly prove your abilities inside the office with a structured system if you hope to be able to achieve success outside of it. You must continue be able to master the basics of sales at the foundational level to be able to grow and create a successful work environment. This could take a year or two, or it could take a decade. In sales, you get what you put in.

Ali said it best when it comes to preparation and its correlation to success:

> *"The fight is won or lost far away from witnesses—behind the lines, in the gym and out there on the road, long before I dance under those lights."*
>
> —MUHAMMAD ALI

A dedicated sales professional needs to be doing much more than arriving at a customer's office or picking up the phone and dialing in hopes that a prospect will buy. This is not the formula for success and never will be. On a microscale, there has always been some luck involved; we all know with enough activity you will come across a prospect that is the perfect fit and has an easy and short sales cycle for you. Enjoy these, but do not expect them. Relying on this type of luck will result in frustration, a short sales career, and a lot of penny-pinching at the beginning of the month when the bills roll in. Instead, understand that 'luck' is where opportunity meets preparation. The more books you consume, podcasts you listen to, blogs you read, and seminars you attend will consistently raise your level of preparation. In sales, especially early in your career, devoting your time away from work to your profession is the greatest investment you can make, and by doing this you will quickly be able to create an environment and working conditions that best fit your life.

IN SALES, TIME DOES NOT EQUAL MONEY

While I was in the process of writing this book, I had many talks with some of my lifelong friends within the sales profession, picking their brains about some of the most important skills they have learned along the way. I wanted to know what they wish they had been told when they were starting, and what lessons they have learned to be true. One of the best pieces of advice I heard was from a friend of mine named David Rothenberger. I am going to paraphrase some of the points that he made along with some direct quotes. However, the gist of it was realizing that in sales "Time does not equal money". Many of you will be entering the sales profession from several different directions, but most of you will be coming from job experiences where things were pretty straight-forward; you were paid an hourly wage. Regardless of how much or how little work you did, you received a set amount of money. It was easy to calculate, and it was easy to decide if it was worth the time and energy you were expending on it. Simply put, time equaled money. This is not the case in sales, as you will most likely be working on one of the commission structures previously outlined.

This is where things can get dicey for a new salesperson in the profession, mainly because you are being dropped into a surrounding where only the strong have survived and continue to thrive. The weak ones who could not cut it have already disappeared. You do not see them in this environment, you are only left with the ones that have passed the first test. Here is how David put it:

"Young sales professionals are entering a business setting where those around them are survivors. Individuals who are in the sales profession for a long period are there because they've achieved a level of success. The people that these new sales professionals don't see are the ones that couldn't make it, those who didn't have the drive, and the ones who were not willing to do what it takes. Be prepared young sales professionals, you will be comparing yourselves to the individuals that remain and thrive, not the ones that have come and gone. In your new career, using analytical reports and company figures, you will need to identify what your company categorizes as success. It will be paramount for you to identify what you need to do to become a survivor and one that thrives.

Weekly sales reports don't show how many hours you put in, how many cold calls you made, or how many good leads you feel you have. The weekly sales reports capture one thing, revenue earned for the company by you! Each dollar of revenue earned is a victory for you. It's a clear figure which is viewed by the sales managers as an indicator of your success. And it is a benchmark for which you can measure your growth, development, and achievement week after week. With this figure you can see if you are successful. It can also illustrate how much more you need to do to be successful within your professional sales setting.

You will need to establish, tailor, and refine your approach to do what it takes to be successful. So, you say to yourself on a Friday afternoon, "I made 20 cold calls this week and put in 45 hours." Okay, what's your contribution on the sales report this week? If it's not good, adjust your approach next week. The following Friday you may say to yourself, "I made 40 cold calls this week and put in 55 hours of work." Thank you for the extra effort, but what's your contribution on this week's sales report? If it's not better than last week, you've got more to do. And it begins, a process that will take you years to establish until you are a respectable contributor to the weekly sales figures. If you are in a sales environment where the sales figures are accessible for your peers to see, everyone is examining your numbers and they are judging you not by the hours you put in, but by that single revenue figure. Remember, count your victories, not your hours.

If you have an expectation early in your career to come into the office on time, make a few calls in the morning, visit a client or two in the afternoon, and be home by 3:30pm because that's what the sales staff who have been around for years are doing, you can forget about that. If you're basing your daily approach on what those around you are doing, you're taking the wrong approach. These people have been in the game for a long time, developed their tactics, established their client relationships, and done what was necessary to become contributors to the revenue figures. You can get there too. You can be one of these established sales reps that appear to have their system dialed in. But that will come with effort and time. If you want to become one of the survivors, the ones that thrive in the sales profession, you need to start by counting your victories, not your hours.

In short, no one cares about how many hours you put in or the volume of cold calls you make, and neither should you. You should care about your victories. In the sales profession, it's all about revenue."

As you can tell, David does not sugar-coat anything. When it comes to the brass tacks of it all, sales are all about results. When you are dropped into a location where you're surrounded by people who have already provided the baseline amount of what is expected, you must be willing to work harder than them, and you must be willing to put in more time while earning less dollars per hour. The managers do not care if it took you 100 hours or if it took you one hour to achieve your weekly or monthly goals, they just expect results.

This is why it is so important to develop a strong foundation based on hard work, good habits, and mental toughness.

To become like the survivors David is discussing, it is crucial to focus on building your own sales process from the ground up, not replicating their exact behaviour that has been honed and personalized to their strengths. In the next part of this book, I am going to tell you about these foundational skills and good habits that all successful sales professionals must master and refine in their early years. Applying these skills from the beginning allows you the opportunity to exponentially increase your rate of success in both the short and long-term.

PART III

WHAT WILL HOLD YOU BACK IN SALES?

FEAR OF REJECTION

R EGARDLESS OF WHAT ASPECT OF life you choose to look at, rejection will be part of it. From relationships and sports to school and career goals, we have all dealt with it in one form or another. Life has a funny way of making a mockery of the best laid plans and intentions. What makes sales different than most situations? Sales professionals are actively seeking rejection. Not literally, but realistically we will be told "no" more than all the other professions combined.

In sales, you will grow to accept this fact, learn to use it during negotiations, and harness it to your advantage in some scenarios. However, at this stage you must accept "no" as part of your new reality. There are many sales books in the market that touch on the topic of rejection and the importance of embracing it.

It's uncomfortable, it's nerve-wracking, and it's scary. It's everything else you can think of to describe it. If you skipped forward to this part of the book hoping I had a magic formula to overcome this—I am sorry to disappoint you—I don't have one. Nobody does. There is good news though; you can overcome it! Anyone can.

The first step is escaping the reality that it can be avoided, the same way the best baseball players fail more often than they succeed. You will be told "no" more often than "yes" daily, and every "no" can be looked at like a dividend received from a stock—something you can take away from the encounter and use as a learning opportunity. In the meantime, as you gain comfort in rejection and develop a thick skin, while you continue to train and implement the other habits that are discussed in these sections. Once you are aware of the different skills you need to work on, you will be able to multi-task and stack these behaviours together.

Every encounter with rejection is going to be different and, most of the time, the best method is to pick the phone back up and go on with your day. If you find yourself being affected by the results of continuous rejection or have a particularly bad encounter, it may be best to walk away for a moment and collect yourself. A quick coffee or water break will usually do the trick.

The key is, no matter what happens or how you feel about it, always keep moving forward. Keep focused on your goals and don't let somebody having a bad day, bad week, heck, bad life, affect you for longer than it should. Remember, after you finish your interaction with that individual, they have already forgotten about you; don't let their actions reside with you either. The moment you understand that this has happened to everybody who has ventured into the world of sales, and that you realize it was nothing personal towards you, the sooner you will start seeing more results. Realize that this will also help you grow from a personal standpoint, not just in sales. Always remember, the only way to overcome this is to continue to pick up the phone and call on the next prospect. I understand this is easier said than done but know that success is only achieved beyond the fear of rejection.

EXCUSES

"I can't reach this person", "I can't get through their gatekeeper", "This person will never buy", "I've tried to sell to them before, they won't buy". Don't get me started on some of the things I've heard around a sales office. The list goes on and on. My goodness, if you spend enough time in a negative environment, you will wonder how anything has ever been sold to anyone!

This is another section that I believe is transferable to different segments in life; excuses are the main difference between successful people and quitters, winners and losers, champions and participants. Winners take the first step, even when they don't know where they will end up or how long the journey will take. They venture out of their comfort zone and create their own success. In sales, when you can think of

100 reasons not to do something, let the one reason to do it rise to the top and guide you.

The fact that you're reading this book means you have already started to take the steps needed to succeed. Right now, you could be doing any number of other things with your time. Instead, you're focusing on your goals and learning about what is needed to be successful. Realize that no salesperson is exempt from making excuses to protect themselves from something they are afraid of. You will make them to rationalize why you didn't make a sale, why you didn't make a call, why you didn't follow up with that prospect who was not receptive the last time you spoke with them. In reality, you know you should be doing these things and learning from the situation. Ask yourself what you could do differently next time to have a more favourable outcome.

Unfortunately, your ego does not like to be bruised. It will go to great lengths to prevent this, and a timely excuse allows unfavourable outcomes and actions to be justified. The sooner you push your ego aside and stop yourself from making these excuses, the quicker you will begin to hold yourself personally accountable, allowing you to succeed at a much faster rate than excuses ever will.

In a sales environment, when those around you are struggling, you will realize the meaning of "misery loves company". They would much prefer you to be struggling as well—this helps reinforce the idea that it's an outside factor preventing their success. A much easier pill to swallow. Do not let these outside factors manifest in your own thought process. Instead, see through this negativity, and even in the worst-case scenario, you will have gained a learning experience by facing the situation head on and coming out the other side. Learn from it, ask colleagues what you could have done differently, talk to your manager about the situation, and discuss how you can improve moving forward. Development in the sales industry lies in the places where you're uncomfortable. Things are not given to you in this career, they are earned.

BELIEF IN THE PRODUCT

I understand that believing in the product may seem more fitting in the "pro" category of selling. And yes, belief in the product is a valuable and necessary attribute when selling any goods or service. However, there are more factors that need to coincide with this belief to create true success. Conversely, not having full and unequivocal belief in your product can be the key piece that completely derails you. You will never have the ability to fully commit yourself to the product and company without this belief; missing this element will always hold you back from reaching your full potential.

Zig Ziglar, one of my all-time favourite sales authors and presenter instilled the importance of belief in me. Integrity is a vital characteristic of any individual, especially a salesperson. Belief in the product is a major step in ensuring this personal integrity to yourself and to your customers. If you are motivating a prospect to spend their hard-earned money on a product or service that you stand behind, you better be sure that you do so with full confidence, honesty, and belief. If you're not willing to use it, why should they?

Obviously, you may be in an environment where you are selling something that you can't afford or does not apply to your current situation. However, you best be sure that if you had the money, as your prospects do, that you would choose your product over the competitors if given the same information. If you sell Honda cars and drive a Toyota, why should your customers trust you? If you sell Coke and drink Pepsi, why should your customer listen to you? Practice what you preach; find a product that inspires you, find something you're passionate about and let that show through when you talk to prospects. If you do not feel your product provides the most VALUE for your customers, then find the one that you feel does, and sell that. Your customers will sense your lack of belief in a product; they will hear it in your voice, and they will see it on your face.

Looking back at my first sales job, I can fully connect with the importance that belief in the product can have. I was selling car wax, and I didn't even own a vehicle. As previously mentioned, I would sit and wait for cars to pull up and people to start filling their tank, then I would spring into action. From a timing perspective, I had from the start of the person pumping gas in their car until the moment they paid to introduce myself, demo the product, overcome objectives, and try to close the sale. Talk about a short sales cycle.

I was green when it came to sales and looking back, I had a whole lot to learn. However, I had one thing going for me, I loved the product! Even though I didn't own a car, I would constantly save my demonstration canisters and even bought new ones from the company. When I visited home, I gave them to family and friends, and would help them apply it to their vehicles. When I performed my demonstrations, my enthusiasm would shine through (Pun intended). If I was not willing to showcase it on my parents' vehicle because I was worried about the results, then I did not deserve to be selling it to strangers.

I had a lot of rough edges to smooth in sales before I was able to start making money selling the product, but without the belief in it, I would never have even gotten off the ground. By the end of the summer, I was a top sales rep in the region and was able to learn valuable sales lessons along the way. If you do not fully believe in your product, you will not reach your full potential in sales.

YOU AND YOUR SELF-DOUBT

When I began pondering about writing this book and outlining some of the topics I wanted to discuss, I told myself that there were individuals out there who would benefit from learning what I have been through in my career. I knew that if one person was able to connect with these concepts and transfer this information to jump start their sales career, then it would be worth it. However, I started to doubt myself. I wondered if I could really help someone and what it is that I could offer them. I asked myself if I had time to write a book and if so, would that time be better spent towards investing in my current career or on a different project.

These thoughts delayed my early progression. I started and stopped multiple times, put the project off on more than one occasion, and doubted my own knowledge. It took time, but I realized that if I could commit to researching and putting my best foot forward to share my stories and experience with those who needed it, it would exemplify exactly what I am trying to portray in this section. The only thing stopping me was myself.

The fact that this book has found its way into your hands means that I was able to fight through the excuses and negativity, leave my comfort zone, and lead by example. If I was not willing to listen and adhere to my own advice, why would I deserve your time and attention? I wouldn't. I know how detrimental your own personal thoughts and biases can be towards your own success and wellbeing. It's important to understand the control that it can have over you and learning to navigate this in a positive manner as quickly as possible will allow you to flip this negative and use it to your advantage.

Motivation, both intrinsic and extrinsic is by far the most powerful stimulus of production one can harness. Unfortunately, it can also be the most detrimental and self-doubting emotion if you are not able to capture it. The finicky part about motivation is that it varies so vastly between individuals. If someone was able to find an all-in-one motivating formula for everyone, they would be one wealthy individual and we would have a very productive society. Everyone would be fit, succeeding in their dream job, waking up at 5am, and be the epitome of their best self. Obviously, this isn't the case.

So, as an individual, you need to find what works for you. Is it external? Family, money, fame, attraction from others, accolades, and awards? Is it internal? Feeling gratification, achieving your personal best, striving to better yourself, the feeling of accomplishment? In the end, it doesn't matter. If you're able to find out what works for you and release it in a positive manner, you will achieve more than you ever thought possible. When it comes to motivation, the secret recipe will differ with each individual; this is for you to discover and, ultimately, maximize. This will take time for you to figure out, as the proper combination of motivators may not always be the obvious choice and may change over time. Though I don't have the answer for you, I can tell you what worked for me, and has continued to work for me moving forward.

It is important to remember that there can be many motivators present at any given time. In fact, the more motivators that are in sync at once, the better. However, there will always be a core motivator that you can fall back on, especially if times get tough. If you stripped away your secondary and tertiary motivators, it would be a setback, but you could keep working and fighting. When you identify this core motivation, its power cannot be described. It gets you out of bed in the morning, it gets you to work every day, and it keep your eyes set on the future and not looking back.

For me, I found my core motivation internally. I have a colourful background in sports, and I have been lucky enough to play high levels of baseball and hockey and had the privilege of playing four years of university-level football. Early in my sports career, being from a small town the talent pool was naturally a little easier to excel. This gave me the opportunity to move on to higher levels of competition with a much higher level of talent. This is where I first learned the true value of motivation and dedicating myself to the sport.

Being naturally competitive, I had flirted with moments of surface motivation throughout my life, but committing to play the sport at the highest level required me to search for motivation to a deeper degree. When I arrived at university, I was not particularly good compared to the players around me, on my first day of spring camp, I was fourth on the depth chart at my position. I was disappointed, of course, and I was angry as I felt I did not get a fair shot. As time passed, I realized I was not as talented as the players in front of me and my positioning was justified. I had never had to work harder than those around me to be better, I had never had to find motivation to become better than my natural talent in order to maximize my potential. Well guess what... if I wanted to play, I would have to work harder to succeed. I had found something worth fighting for, something that I wanted, and something that would not be given to me if I did not put in more effort than those around me.

If I wanted it, I had to take it! Just writing that gets me amped up; it works for me whether I am talking about sales, sports, or life. I am intrinsically motivated by the idea of being my best self. I hate wasted potential. I understand that I won't be the best at every endeavour I pursue, but it will not be because I did not work hard enough for it.

The same attitude applies for sales. I hate hearing that another salesperson has had a better day, week, month, or year than me. Do not confuse this for being jealous of their accomplishments or demeaning a colleague. It means that

I am not the best at what I'm doing and that I need to get better. This result can happen for any number of reasons: less experience, less knowledge on the product, bad timing, etc. However, most of the time, the likely scenario is that the better salesperson, achieved the better results. Obviously, this is not always the case, but over time and with more data extrapolated, more often than not, the best will rise to the top.

I always look at this as an opportunity to improve. I will talk in more detail about mentors and working with the best people in your company later in the book. For now, just realize that when you notice people who are better at what they do than you, this is the perfect opportunity to learn how they got to where they are. It should also remind you that if they are able to accomplish this, there is no reason why you can't either.

To get back to the main point, in sales I am motivated to be the best. If I am not, I do everything in my power to become the best. Even though the financial benefits and quota are great by-products and work as secondary motivators, I want to become the best because I personally feel I have the ability to be. This success does not happen overnight, as developing good sales skills and being a consistent salesperson takes time and patience. However, if you believe you have the internal motivation and belief in yourself like I do, then you can achieve this. If I simply do not attempt to be great out of laziness, lack of desire, self-doubt, or mediocrity, then I am wasting my potential. You know how I feel about that—I hate it.

I am very passionate about this topic because I truly feel this is one of the main reasons I have been able to find success in sales, and why I have yet to settle in my career. I also recognize that failure to find proper motivation can completely derail your career. Seeing talented people wasting their potential through lethargy or a sense of entitlement is something I have never associated myself with nor do I want to. These are toxic habits that can slowly creep into your own if you allow them to. The challenge for you is to find out what your motivation is; find the reason you swing your feet out of bed and get ready every morning. If you already know what your motivation is – great—use it! If you don't know, that's okay too. Keep looking for it and when you do find it, harness it, and let it propel you! Allow your motivation to be the driving force that thrusts you to commit to your ambitions.

Before I end this sections, know that this is not something you're going to feel every day. You're going to have your bad days, your slow days, and the ones where you need the extra cup of coffee. This is about consistency, creating positive habits, and attaining long and short-term goals that you're striving for. This is not a rah-rah speech about waking up at 5am every day, jogging a mile before breakfast and then conquering the world. A bad day does not mean that you need to start over. You're human, just pick yourself up the next day and get back at it.

PART IV

HOW TO EXCEL IN SALES

THERE IS AN IMPORTANT REASON why I wrote about what will hold you back in sales before I dove into the details on how to excel in them. Sales does not have a cheat code; you do not get to fast forward to the good parts. You don't get to skip ahead to an increased bank account, having your name at the top of the sales chart, and enjoying all the other benefits that come with mastering the craft of sales. Before you move forward and excel, you first need to correct your poor habits and behaviours, as well as overcome the fears that are holding you back.

You must dig out the weeds before you plant the flowers.

Once again, I come to you with experience when I say I have witnessed first-hand the power of these positive habits and skills. I have observed people around me propel their careers right in front of my eyes. Unfortunately, it also took me longer than it should have to realize these traits. I was forced to learn these lessons through trial and error until I stubbornly admitted to myself they were part of the process and not something that I could bypass. It took future reflection to realize these patterns were associated with the success. I ask that you learn from my trials and tribulations and immediately start implementing these strategies and habits into your routine so that you can accelerate your path to success and begin achieving your goals.

Trial by Fire

Simple and straight forward. In sales, you cannot stand on the sidelines, dip your toe in the water, or wait for success to come to you. You need to put yourself out there, be vulnerable, and take risks. Understand that the results of falling on your face and embarrassing yourself is a lesson learned in itself and a step forward. Do not perceive this as a negative. Early on, you will learn more from these failures than you will from any amount of accidental success. The fact that you're able to take that first step off the ledge is proof in itself that you're capable of making it in this profession.

It's like jumping into the lake when you know the water is cold, after you overcome the initial shock, the end result is worth it. In this career, you fail, and fail, and fail again until it pushes you to the limit. The important factor is to both learn from your disappointments and improve yourself for next time. You're going to encounter failure regardless of when you start, so you might as well start facing it on day one. Waiting on the inevitable will only delay your progress and build up anxiety within yourself. The Navy Seals have a saying "Get comfortable being uncomfortable", and if you want to succeed in this profession you need to live outside of your comfort zone.

Overcome 'Worst Case Scenario'

This is essentially an extension of the Trial by Fire section and can also be described as a case of the "what ifs". The "what ifs" can prevent even the most capable salespeople from picking up their phone or knocking on the prospect's door. The best way to describe this medical case is: the fear a salesperson has imagining all of the responses a prospect MIGHT have. What if the prospect is busy? What if the prospect is annoyed at me? What if the prospect doesn't like me, what if….what if…what if. Honestly, the possibilities are as endless as your imagination.

The biggest thing to remember is that the actual worst-case scenario is "No". Sure, the prospect may add a few extra words in there, and, if you've been doing it long enough, there may even be some that are explicit. In the end, whether it's polite or obscene, the answer is still just a "No". By this point in the book, you should realize that this should not be looked at as a negative. This means that you put yourself out there, you made yourself vulnerable, and you attempted to sell your product to a customer. Obviously, you would have preferred a sale, but now you have some tangible experience to work with in order to improve yourself and be better on your next call. You will have also heard another objection that you can work on for when it presents itself again in the future. Without picking up the phone and overcoming your worst-case scenario fears, you will not develop the building blocks needed to gain experience and come one step closer to making a sale.

To many, this can be the hardest fear to overcome in the sales profession. The reason for this is simple; there is so much information at our fingertips with the internet and our electronic devices. Some salespeople attempt to learn everything about their prospect, their company, their market, etc. By doing so, they delay actually contacting the prospect to learn about them through conversation.

Although this will differ with each scenario, the goal is to find balance. Try to think of it as a first date- it's nice to know a little bit about them beforehand so that you have some talking points, but you don't need to know their life story. It's helpful to be able to get the conversation going and then learn more about the prospect organically by listening and asking good questions based on their responses. It also prevents you from making assumptions before actually speaking with them. The irony of dedicating so much research to a specific prospect is that you can take all this time to learn everything you can about a customer, only to find that they won't give you the time of day to speak. They may have just recently bought something, have no budget, or just generally not be interested. Now you've spent all this time researching, only to find out your time could have been better spent elsewhere. If you had just picked up the phone or knocked on the door to start, you would have saved yourself time and already moved on to your next prospect.

Another definition of this is paralysis by analysis. The best solution is to revert back to trial by fire. It can be difficult to look at the bigger picture when you're staring at a lead. Just know that learning good habits and rewiring the detrimental behaviours discussed in the previous sections are far more important early on than actually getting the sale. I repeat, learning good habits and bypassing bad behaviours that slow the progress of new sales reps is more important than the sale itself. Sounds crazy, right? Let me give you a hypothetical situation to help explain this. Think of it as learning to hit a golf ball. I'll give you two different scenarios. You are given fifty golf balls, and the goal is to be able to consistently hit the ball straight by the end of them.

Scenario #1

You begin to hit the golf balls and, as expected, they are flying all over the place. Some go to the left, some go to the right, and some just dribble off the tee. You hit a couple more and all of sudden you smack one right down the middle. You're not sure how you did it, but it doesn't really matter because that's the result you were looking for. You hit a few more and they continue to fly in all different directions as you try to correct what you're doing wrong on your own. All of sudden, SMACK, you hit another one right down the middle. Your confidence builds, as you think you must be doing something right. This continues for some time, but by the time you're done, you've only hit about four or five nice ones, with no consistency on your other forty-five. You're just hoping you randomly put it all together on each shot, with no real rhyme or reason. When all is said and done, you have accomplished what you wanted a few times, but you have yet to learn how you did it. If you were asked to hit another fifty, you would be no closer to your goal now than you were when you started.

Scenario #2

You seek out some guidance and ask for a little help getting started. A considerate individual decides to give you some tips and points you in the right direction. Before even thinking of smacking it down the fairway like you want to do, they tell you to focus on keeping your head down, eyes on the ball, and try not to over swing. Things start off slow for you- the ball is shooting in every direction and you even completely whiff on some. This frustrates you, as you see others hitting a few down the middle while you struggle. Your mentor continues to preach the fundamentals and constructively tweaks some of the mistakes you've made in past attempts. Slowly but surely, your swing begins to take shape. You may not be hitting them right down the middle, but you're consistently keeping it close, and fundamentals are becoming habit. The coaching is becoming more specific as you make less mistakes. By the time you make it to your 30th ball, you've already hit one or two down the middle and now you're starting to hit them further and more accurate than the people around you. Even though some of people had some good shots before you, they did not learn the fundamentals of how they were doing it, and they are still making noticeable mistakes and growing increasingly frustrated. By the time you finish your fifty golf balls, you are ready to start learning how to chip and putt, instead of still struggling with how to hit the ball straight. Flatten the learning curve and expedite long-term results.

For those of you who are not golfers, that's okay. In summary, take the time to learn the basics of sales before you worry about making a sale on every call. The goal is to build a career and make sales on a consistent basis, more than it is to make the first sale.

Create Good Habits Outside of Work

Although I touched on the topic of habits in the previous section, I wanted to build on it further to help you fully understand how to balance them. As you will see, this is a combination of work and life habits that I find extremely important. This is certainly not a self-help book, but the habits you create must be consistent away from your work life to help better the effectiveness of them with your career. Habits are not a switch that you turn on and off, and will have a major correlation in your success if you find ways to incorporate them into all aspects of your life. There are plenty of excellent examples of good habits that are not mentioned that will benefit you, but I did not want to dilute the list. I sought to ensure that I added the most important ones that I've found to be extremely beneficial to myself, as well as ones suggested to me by other sales professionals.

Organization

Take the time to organize your living space and your office space. There is no way that you'll be able to do one if you don't do the other. Organization is an all-the-time thing. If you can't find where you put things in your living space, there's a good chance you're misplacing things at work. If you miss a dentist appointment because you forgot to write it down or put it in your calendar, there's a good chance you're going to forget to mark down your meeting or phone call with a prospect. Take the time to write important information down, review your calendar at the beginning of each week and at the start of each day. There's a very good chance your company will have a customer relationship management (CRM) software to help with these items. If it does, learn it as best you can and use it to your advantage. Make sure you don't miss important dates and times both at work and in your personal life. Being punctual will net you sales AND ensure you get to your kids' soccer games on time.

Physical Activity

You might think this is something that comes natural for me, given my background in competitive sports. However, when I started my career in the business world, my lifestyle immediately became sedentary. My athletic frame quickly became pudgy, lazy, and over-caffeinated. As someone who was told they were "born for sales", I was struggling with my new job. I was having difficulty learning new sales concepts, and making mistakes like the ones discussed in previous sections. Post-university, I started in inside sales, which meant being on the phone and at a desk for eight hours a day. After a year, I had gained at least twenty-five extra pounds; I was rarely active and clinging to my glory days of being a former athlete. Most days, my energy came from coffee and sugar, and the best way to describe me would have been languid. My only saving grace at this time was that, no matter how low my energy was and what struggles I faced, my motivation to succeed was still a driving force. I continued to learn and apply good sales techniques that I picked up along the way. Unfortunately, I sacrificed my physical health while I was doing it.

Then came a turning point in my sales career and post athletic life. I was tired of how I felt, how I looked, and how I was treating myself. I had one of those rock bottom moments when I saw myself in the mirror. I recalled my previous physique and saw that it had slowly become bogged down in many places without notice and my confidence had plummeted. This continued to fester within me for another week as I continued to work.

Finally, this sentiment erupted within me and I had had enough. I signed back up at my gym and began an active regiment. As expected, the transformation was slow at first, but I kept it consistent. After about eight weeks without really seeing any difference in my physical appearance, the changes that I was noticing within myself were astonishing. Most importantly, I was benefiting from having far more energy during the day. This could be attributed to both the physical activity and the fact I was eating better to feed an active body instead of a lazy one. Unbeknownst to me, my confidence had grown to a point one of my managers noted it. He told me I sounded stronger on the phone, and was more talkative around the office. The best part was that my sales were climbing at the same time.

I'm not saying that going to the gym or staying active away from work is going to make you a good salesperson-that is not the parallel here. However, when you become lazy and dormant in an office job, you are not your best self. And when you are not your best self in sales, the repercussions are frustration, declining motivation, and poor performance. Unfortunately, this can happen very quickly and, if this is your first office job, it's a new version of the 'freshman fifteen' for adults. Since the day I had that brazen conversation with myself in the mirror, I have not looked back. I promise you, this is the best thing you can do for yourself away from the office. If down the road in your sales career you find yourself in a rut, please remember the difference this can make for you in your life and in your career.

Sleep

I am not going to dive too deep into this topic, as I think it is pretty self-explanatory. The reason I included it though, is because sleep and physical activity are probably going to be the two habits that are the first to slip. If you are a recent graduate or a young professional, you are probably used to functioning on low amounts of sleep and managing pretty well for yourself. Heck, you could be reading this when you should be sleeping (you can go to bed after you finish this section).

There is no question, you can be successful, motivated, and productive with little sleep. Everyone is different and each person needs to learn their own schedule. Everyone is also in varying situations: some are married, some have children, some care for others, etc. Whatever it is, you can only put sleep on the backburner for so long before it finally catches up to you.

Some people have jobs where they can switch themselves onto autopilot, punch in and punch out, collect their pay and repeat. Salespeople cannot do this. You have to treat each new prospect with the same enthusiasm and excitement for your product as you do the last, regardless of how you feel. If you appear sluggish, unenthusiastic, and uninterested during a pitch with the prospective buyer, they will sense this, and they will have a negative perception of you and your product. This doesn't mean you have to go into every meeting with the eagerness of someone from an infomercial, but you're not yourself when you are running on fumes from a lack of sleep.

If you go too long disregarding proper sleep and proverbially 'burning the candle at both ends' without any corrective measures, then you can run into sleep deprivation and sleep debt. This results in slower cognitive function, the inability to process new information, and trouble recalling previously understood knowledge. This is something you can research yourself, as there is some great information on the topic, but for now just know you can only go so long without the proper amount of sleep until your career and personal life suffer. My advice is to begin creating a proper sleep schedule as soon as you can, especially during the work week.

Turn off Work Mode

For individuals outside of the sales profession, this can be pretty easy to accomplish. They clock out and don't think about work until they show up again the next day. There are also some within the sales industry that don't have a problem checking in and out when the end of the day rolls around. The problem is, as we know, this profession gives back what you put in. You cannot find consistent success by only applying yourself during work hours. When this is the case, you will soon find yourself falling behind your colleagues and underperforming. If you want to be successful, you have to be working hard during work hours and then working even harder away from the office, especially in your first few years.

I offer you plenty of different options in an upcoming sections to help you continue your growth after you have finished this book and implemented the lessons learned. This reminder is for the people who are truly committed to being their best self in the profession and will actually find it difficult to turn off work mode. The people who need this reminder are going to be the ones who ultimately uncover success in sales.

The key is to understand the delicate balance of continued growth and avoiding burnout. You cannot spend your entire time away from the office consumed with work; you need to actively find hobbies to take your mind off the emotional strain that this profession can create. Use the organizational skills discussed earlier to dedicate time for yourself to spend with family and friends, attend sporting events, concerts, and entertainment functions. It can be anything that you enjoy that does not involve work in any way. The results are even better if this time is spent without looking at your phone. Most people are already addicted to their devices as is, and in business, this is magnified even more. Your work will typically involve constant phone calls and emails and, depending on your schedule and the industry, they can be coming in at all hours of the day. Unless you're a doctor, there's a good chance you don't need to have your phone on you at all times and the emails and return calls can wait until you're finished with whatever it is you're doing to spend your free time.

Keep in mind, if you are someone that is used to a 9-5 check in/check out schedule, you may need to find a balance in the other direction. Set aside time to read sales books, industry news, and blogs. Learn when to relax and when to strengthen your craft. This reminder is geared towards the highly motivated people that are doing everything they can to improve themselves in sales. Take a break, relax, decompress, re-energize yourself and then get right back to crushing it!

Learn Your Product and Industry

For many of us, when we take on our first sales job, we are entering into an industry that we are unfamiliar with. This can create uneasiness for some people, but this is something that comes with the territory. Most good companies will provide adequate training to help guide new hires in the right direction. They will teach you the basics of the product or service, the industry, the target market, and their expectation of how to represent the company by following their policies and standards. This is obviously a very generic overview as companies will vary greatly on how much training they provide and how specific the training is.

The differentiating factor on which new sales reps excel quickly is based on how much extra work they are willing to put in behind the scenes to expand on these basics taught in the classroom. Ask for extra material to take home and study. Research the company that you work for, the product you offer, the industry you work in, the people you will be speaking to, etc. If you are following the habits provided earlier in this sections like trial by fire and overcoming fears, you will quickly run into objections about your product or company from prospective customers.

First off and most importantly, understand that there is no shame in not knowing an answer to a customer's question or stumbling when you are faced with an objection you did not expect. This is an excellent learning opportunity and, when dealt with correctly, will enable you to perform better the next time you are faced with a similar situation. My go-to response has always been, "That's a great question! Let me find out for you".

When you put in the extra effort to learn as much as you can about your company and industry, you will acquire a wealth of knowledge for your customers and build a trust that can be difficult to find in today's business world. The sooner you are able to quickly and accurately overcome objections, the faster you will be able to put yourself into the next step of the sales cycle, and ultimately start closing business for yourself. This is a stage in your sales development that is not without its frustrating moments, but one that, when improved upon, will jump start your career. You will learn these details on the job as you fail, correct yourself, and then try again. These traits are all best learned through experience but putting in extra work to learn finite details about your product and industry that will springboard you past other new sales representatives.

If you wanted to learn how to sell at the pace of a snail, you would not be reading this book. Go from Padewan to Jedi through the guidance of Yoda (Or beginner to expert for all of the non-Star Wars fans) as quickly as possible.

Sell More Than the Product

Like most of the topics in this book, this was one of the major factors that stunted my original progression in sales. As backwards as it sounds, early success in any sales job can be a double-edged sword. The obvious benefits are confidence, commissions, and a positive association for the career of sales. However, it can create a trap by allowing to you to believe there is only one way to sell a product. Metaphorically speaking, there's more than one way to cook an egg; if all you know is scrambled, then you are isolating yourself from a large sector of potential buyers.

One of the most important things you can learn as a seller is that people buy a product for a variety of different reasons. Instead of selling them on why YOU think they should be buying it, sell them on why THEY should be buying it. This is why it is important to be attentive early in your career and pay attention to the variety of different selling strategies used by individuals within your company. In light of this, fight the instinct to continue selling your product the exact same way all the time. The more you learn about your potential customers, the more you can streamline your pitch and conversation towards what they desire in the product. This will lead to long-term success and more satisfied customers.

The concept of this book is not to go through the different ways to sell a specific product; there are plenty of great books which will be listed later to help guide you through that process as you build your experience. Use your early days at the company to learn about different characteristic of your product(s). Some examples include features, benefits, price, value, service, prestige, efficiency, technology advancement, effectiveness, etc. Utilize your full arsenal of information to sell specifically to each customers' needs.

Find Something You Are Passionate About Selling

As you may or may not have noticed, all of the habits provided to help you excel in sales are designed to build off of one another. This topic is no different, but it is also a little trickier to explain as it is subjective and more personal to each reader. Everyone will have a different expectation within their job when deciding whether or not it is a proper fit for them. With this in mind, I am going to touch on the key factors that I looked for when I was trying to find the right fit for myself within the sales profession.

As noted many times, I have gone down a rocky path trying to find my way through the clutter in order to find a position that I really felt comfortable in. The experience of these ups and downs has been the primary motivation that inspired me to write this book. Understanding the emotional highs and lows of the beginning stages of a sales career can be a difficult when you haven't experienced them first-hand. I have attempted to encapsulate these learning curves and transitions throughout this book. In the beginning, had I learned to perform in a more efficient way, I'm certain that I would be much further ahead in my career or reached where I am today sooner, but I digress.

To fully understand this subsection, I want you to realize that finding a passion in what you sell does not necessarily mean that you have to sell a product or service that you can't live without or are infatuated with. Obviously, this helps, but as you will see, there is more to it than that. To me, there have always been a few key factors that helped me understand if I had found passion in what I was selling. Even before the product or service itself, I am of the opinion that, first and foremost, you must believe in the company you are working for. When your vision and personal beliefs align with the company you work for, you build a foundation that makes it difficult to fail. This can range from a large corporation to a small business. If you find yourself wanting to both work for your own personal goals, as well as those of the company, then you will have a solid base to build on.

Secondly, for me, the product is the next most important aspect in the process. Take the time to educate yourself on the product and how it compares with others in the industry. That way, you can decide if you believe in the company and what they offer to their customers. If you do not believe in the product and how it is delivered, then you will never be able to sell it. The best way to decide on this aspect is to think "if I were in the position of the customer, would I buy this product or would I buy the competitor's?" If the answer is not the company you work for, you might as well find a new job right now; heck, you can even go work for the competitor if you think their product offers a better value. Once you believe that you have the best product, or at least the best value in the industry, it is now time to learn as much as you can about it and how it will help your customers.

The third factor is the office environment and culture. This includes managers, co-workers, and everyone in between. This can be the most ambiguous of all the factors, mainly because there are many different personalities, and I can't be certain as to which one you, the reader, fall into. Just know that the people you work with are going to have a major influence in how well you excel within the profession, as well as how fast you progress through the learning curve of sales. Early in your career, the co-workers and managers within your workplace are going to help mold your sales style, and will either encourage you to develop healthy positive sales habits or bring you down with negative, debilitating behaviours that will hold you back. Embrace the positivity and quickly block out the toxicity that can exist within an organization.

If you're reading this, the good news is, I am doing my best to guide you with a roadmap to help you recognize red flags within an organization. This should prevent you from slipping into poor habits and should help you recognize, not only those who are successful, but also understanding why it is they are successful. The second piece of good news is that when you're starting out, you are a clean slate. With a fresh palate, you have the ability to learn, absorb, mimic, and mold your own niche within the profession. The most important piece of information I can offer you when it comes to the people you work with is that they each have something unique to offer you, even if that unique piece of information is showing you a behaviour you don't want to replicate.

As I previously discussed in this book, you will meet every different type of personality you can think of in this profession all with their own different perspective, style, routine, and sense of self. However, in general, we all have the same desire; to make more sales, earn a living, and to achieve the goals that we are motivated by. It is important that you find like-minded people within your office that have similar goals, aspirations, and common interests. This is important for not only your work success, but also your own well-being. We spend so much time in our workplace that if it is not enjoyable, it will wear on you. Selling a product you believe in, with people you enjoy being around, for a company you are happy to be associated with, is a powerful combination.

Even with all of this in place, you will inevitably run into managers with different personalities and approaches that differ from your own. This doesn't mean they're wrong, it just means that they're different than you. When you start out, many will attempt to fill your head with different tidbits of knowledge, advice, tips, and tricks. The goal is to filter out the garbage and absorb the gold, then take this information and begin to mold your own style. Unfortunately, some managers can be short-sighted and attempt to fit square pegs into round holes, with little range in their managerial skills. Just know, a destination can have many different roads leading to it; a sales career is not structured like a maze on the back of the children's menu with only one correct path.

In these situations, it is important to stay open-minded and listen to what an individual has to say, as they may drop some inspiring information on you at any given time. If used correctly, this information can be incorporated effectively within your own style. In order to maximize your success, you must be willing to learn from all of the people that you encounter throughout your career. Just because a individual, fundamentally, may be different than you or approaches their career differently than you do, does not mean you cannot find common ground in some sales practices.

Lastly, you need to believe in the **solution** that you are providing to the end user. This final element ties everything together and reverts back to the point that you don't need to be selling a specific product or service that you are passionate about. If instead, you are selling a solution that you genuinely believe in, then you are set-up for success. If the product you offer provides a resolution to a small business to help them provide for their family, or the service relieves frustration and pain from an individual, you can find pride within this. If the trickle-down effect from your efforts delivers a greater sense of purpose than the commission it provides to you, then you can sell anything. If you can confidently shake hands with the end user knowing their experience with the product, interactions with the company, and customer service all align with what you would personally expect as a customer yourself then you will have found something that you are passionate about.

Find the Right Fit

A widely known quote to any seasoned salesperson states "Sales is the easiest low-paying job, or hardest high-paying job you'll ever have". From this perspective, understand that there will be numerous hurdles and barriers you will come across as you try to carve your own path through this minefield that can be a successful sales career. The point is don't make it harder on yourself than it has to be. Sales is not a one-size-fits-all profession, and you have to be mindful of the fact that you may not find the right company straight out of the gate. This does not mean that you immediately jump ship from a job once it starts to get tough, or when you have a spat with a co-worker or manager. There is nothing wrong with building a little character as you grow. There will always be that one person in the office you don't quite jive with or a policy that you disagree with. Continue to improve yourself in the situation you are in and become a better salesperson and craft your skills. You will find that adversity and difficult situations will help you become more adaptive to new environments, which will in turn help you cultivate additional sales skills.

However, sometimes things just don't work out. It can be attributed to any number of reasons, but sometimes the fit just isn't right. If you can have an honest conversation with yourself and know you've done your best to accommodate for the company while being a model employee, and this respect is not being reciprocated, there is no harm in looking elsewhere and finding a better opportunity. I speak from experience on this point, but as previously touched upon I have always found a way to take an important lesson, skill, or self-improvement from each job I have been at. The most negative of situations, although traumatizing at the time, have helped me to become a better salesperson today.

Find a Mentor

Another extremely important piece of advice I can offer to any new salesperson starting out in this profession is to find a mentor. This is so important that I wish I could write this section in capital letters, but I know how annoying that is to read. The benefit of a mentor is critical for one simple reason: sales is hard. Very hard. When you are starting out in sales, it can be and it will be overwhelming. You are expected to learn quickly, produce results, and show that you are cut out for this profession even when the odds are stacked against you. There is also the important fact that when you start out, you will not be making much money. There is a rush to get your feet wet and to start making a reasonable income so that you're not stuck eating Mr. Noodles for the rest of your life. This can be mentally fatiguing, and a mentor is someone that is going to help guide you through the twists and turns of sales because they personally understand the struggles that you're going through. They, themselves, most likely had a mentor who helped them and want to give back. Actually, I can say with certainty that they had one. In all my years, I've yet to meet a successful salesperson who did not.

The first and most important step to finding a mentor is to apply yourself to your craft. Work hard. Apply the habits you've read in this book, do your best to fight through your fears, and show that you are willing to put in the work to become better. Sales professionals don't have time to mentor someone who is sitting around waiting to be helped. If you aren't willing to apply what you already know, why should they show you more? If you waste their time, they will move on and you will get lost in the shuffle.

Secondly, ask professional and informative questions. Show that you have been working behind the scenes to learn more than what has been taught at a surface level. *Don't pretend to know everything*—Ask intelligent questions about the company you work for, a big customer that the company has, or a major account that you know the individual was a key part in landing. Pick their brain. Sales professionals love to talk about their past success and what value they have brought to the company. Genuinely be interested in what they have to say and what you can learn from their experiences. The more you begin to know about them, the more they will want to learn about you. This will translate into them wanting to help you succeed, and wanting you to grow within the company. It is also important to understand that this will not always be the case. Some people do not want to mentor others, some will be happy staying in their own bubble and growing their own career. Others will test you to see if you are willing to put in the work before they help. Maybe they have been burned in the past by people wasting their valuable time and are waiting for you to earn your stripes. These are all reasonable reactions and, if you come across this, that is no reason to be discouraged. Just keep working hard, keep communicating with others, and eventually your efforts will get noticed.

Lastly, choose your mentors wisely. As amazing as most of the people in the sales profession are, there are also manipulative, devious, and conniving individuals. They will look to take advantage of hardworking newcomers for their own personal gains. They will seem to have your best interests in mind, but in the end, they will just be looking to gain something of value and leave you behind. Unfortunately, there is no way to know when you're being used by one of these individuals. You will have to use your own judgement and trust your 'spidey senses'. If you get an uneasy feeling as to how someone is treating you, don't be afraid to speak with others in the company or talk to people you trust outside of your work place. As helpful and amazing as it is to have a good mentor, dealing with a bad one will slow your progress to a halt and may even taint the entire sales profession for you. This isn't meant to scare you from finding someone, it is simply a warning that not everyone in this profession is trying to help you and wishing for your success. Proceed with caution, but be confident in yourself and your own judgement that you will find a genuine person who is there to help you.

There are many benefits to having a mentor who is a colleague within your workplace. You will be able to approach them with specific questions relating to your product, workplace, company, or industry. However, a mentor can also be found in the form of a person you trust beyond the company walls. This can be an individual with sales experience relating to a different industry, authors and influencers with books, podcasts, and YouTube channels, or anyone that you feel you can relate to and trust in their advice. The key factor is knowing their input is coming from a place that has your best interest at the forefront. Again, have faith in your judgement and show appreciation for their help.

Be Obsessed or Be Average

If this heading sounds familiar, it is because this is the title of the book by the well-known sales author Grant Cardone. I reference him later and refer you to a number of his works in subsequent sections. This book really opened my eyes to several different subjects that personally resonated with me. It helped me to connect a number of different dots in my own life, and that's why I felt compelled to have a sub-section by the same name.

After my sports career ended at age twenty-four, I had failed to find myself 'obsessed' with anything else in my life. For as long as I could remember, I had been an athlete, and not just any athlete, but I considered myself to be elite. I was obsessed with becoming better every day. When I was younger, it did not matter what sport that I was playing; whatever it was, I wanted to be the best player on the team and the best player in the league. Even though this was not always the case, as there were always better players around me, I was always striving to become that player.

This wasn't a switch that flipped one day; it was always in me. I hated to lose, and I was motivated by the risk of failure. This motivation helped push me to become a better athlete and player every season as my career progressed. It gave me the opportunity to succeed at higher levels, eventually making the university football roster. After I accomplished that, being on the roster was not enough, I wanted more playing time, I wanted to be a starter, I wanted more and more and dedicated the time and effort needed to fulfil these desires. I considered this an obsession at the time, and even though it was not always glamourous, I loved it. I continue to stress that untapped potential is the biggest waste any person can leave behind, and this was my way of fulfilling it without regret. It was always easy to stay motivated as I was surrounded by many like-minded teammates, knowing that team success relied on the collective efforts of each individual. Football is the ultimate team sport after all. The reason this background is important is because something strange happened to me after I walked off that field for the final time. I lost my identity, I lost my sense of self, I lost my OBSESSION.

The term student-athlete implies that while competing on the gridiron, I also had to attend university classes at the same time. Luckily for me, failure was not an option in any walk of life, so regardless of whether I enjoyed it or not, I could always find the motivation to attend class (most of them), complete assignments, and pull the occasional all-nighter to finish papers or cram before an exam. School was important to me, but it was not an obsession. When all the dust settled, I was an above-average student and that was good enough for me. I do wonder about what types of grades I could have accomplished if I had the same passion for school as I did for sports. I will never know, but I certainly feel like it speaks volumes to how powerful an obsession can become. I attended and graduated university to prevent failure. I grew and fulfilled my potential in football because I was obsessed.

The problem is, as the years passed and my sports career faded in the rear-view mirror, I found myself acting on fear of failure over desire to succeed. I dedicated myself to sales to get by and pay the bills. There was enough intrinsic motivation to be better than some of my colleagues but not enough to strive to be the best. Throughout this stage of my life, I found myself drifting further away from who I thought I was, and whom I had identified myself as for my whole life. Even though I had a steady income, upgraded my living space, became more independent than I had ever been, and had all of the freedom to forge any path that I wanted, the fire was still not lit.

When I was a student-athlete, I was broke—and I mean BROKE. I was calling home monthly asking my mom for grocery money and to help with the bills. I had no free time balancing football, meetings, practice, workouts, school, and trying to have some sort of social life. I was in a dumpy basement apartment, with multiple roommates, and taking side jobs whenever I could to earn a few more dollars. The crazy part is- I loved it. I only realized this several years later, but I loved it because I had one goal in mind, one desire, one obsession. I wanted to become a better football player to help my team win a championship. Obviously graduating was something that I took pride in accomplishing, but it was not my daily passion. Football was my four-course gourmet meal, and school was the sink full of dishes. One needed to be completed out of necessity and the other was where I dedicated my time and effort.

To bring this full circle, the reason I had been struggling since my playing career ended was because I had never redefined my goals. I didn't allow myself to reflect and pursue the next stage of my life. I was, by no means, living in the past as I knew that phase was over. Looking back, I was in a state of purgatory, simply going through the motions.

Finally, seeking a fresh start I moved to a new city and started with a new company. I personally created a set of life goals that I wanted to reach by the time I hit 30. At the time, this gave me about two years, so they were relatively short-term goals, but ones that I was very serious about achieving. I wasn't sure if I would be able to reach them all, I ended up hitting two of the three, but I held myself 100% accountable in an attempt to attain all three. After I reached the age of thirty, I wrote down a number of new goals that I set out to accomplish over the next five years.

If you're reading or listening to this book, it means that I will have completed at least one of these goals. If you would like to know more about what my goals were/are, feel free to reach out to me and I would be happy to share mine and help you with yours. Although this may seem simple enough, it was a major turning point in my life. Anyone can scribble some arbitrary goals on a pad of paper and move on from it, but it takes a different mindset to put thought into major goals that you would like to meet and then altering your routine to match the effort and expectations needed to achieve them.

The reason I credit Grant Cardone for unleashing this potential and perspective in me is, until I read this book, I had never understood how to express the way I felt. He seemed to be able to explain this perfectly and it resonated with me immediately. It helped me connect all of the dots on my timeline. When you're obsessed with goals, the other aspects of your life are white noise. Small annoyances and disruptions no longer distract you, and you'll find ways to maneuver around them as you continue on your path. That's why I didn't care when I was broke but still attaining my goal, and not happy when I had more financial security and stability.

The next piece that really opened my eyes and took me to the next level was when Grant explained that you can have multiple obsessions to allow yourself not to be key holed into a certain mindset. You can be multi-dimensional to allow for growth in multiple aspects of your life. Full potential is only achieved when all facets of life are moving in unison. An engine can only operate when all of the cylinders are firing together. After reading this book, I immediately updated my goals for the age of thirty-five as I realized that, up until this point in my life, my goals had only been singularly focused. I needed to refocus my attention on being obsessed with all the branches of my life. My updated goals included: monetary, physical, real estate, family, and personal. This is a mindset that I had yet to harness until it was presented to me in the proper format.

Think of a 5-tool player in baseball; they are elite in every detail of the game: contact, power, speed, fielding, and arm strength. Average is not in their arsenal. It has taken a tremendous amount of effort and perseverance to hone their skills in all aspects with the same dedication and commitment to each facet. This mindset is no different; the same way an athlete becomes a 5-tool player, you can become a 5-tool person. Heck, why stop there? Why not fifteen tools? You won't look back after you realize the potential of this.

The side effect of having a wider spread of goal means you will have much less free time. It causes you to put your goals into perspective to see if you really are obsessed. Do you decide to binge watch another TV show, or are you going to the gym after work? Do you decide to scan social media, or do you pick up the phone to reach out to another lead? Do you save your money for the newest gadget, or invest it for retirement or a down payment? As your goals become dialed-in and more specific it becomes easier to stay focused, and everyday decisions that direct you towards your goals become the norm. Your obsessions become your obsession. It's a mindset that is hard to describe until you obtain it. You will then find yourself hitting a state of flow that allows you to continue to point your sails in the right direction day after day.

I recognize that this is a deep topic, but one that I am very passionate about. I understand that the readers of this book will all be at different stages of their life as they read this. However, this does not change the message behind it. You could be fresh out of school and trying to find the right career path, or middle-aged and trying to reinvent yourself in a new profession. Regardless of your situation, you need to find something that you're obsessed with in order to move forward each day.

Originally, I personally never became obsessed with sales in particular. No—instead I set a financial goal for myself to hit by thirty-five years old. The number itself is arbitrary, but I know the only way that I can reach it is to become as educated in sales as I possibly can. I listen to audiobooks while driving and read other sales books at night. I pick the brain of co-workers and ask my mentors and bosses for help whenever I feel I have something I can learn from them. Becoming better at sales was just the path I needed to take to get to my goals. Since then, for me, the art of sales has become an obsession in itself.

Even if you are not fully committed to the sales profession in your long-term career plans, the least you could do is fully commit to it while you're here. You may be surprised when you find out the potential you discover within yourself. If you have picked up this book with every intention of making sales your profession, you will have every opportunity to make your own path and reach your goals regardless of how lofty they are. However, it takes this commitment to get your momentum going, and one of the first major obstacles to avoid is falling into a mundane routine because you don't have an identity for yourself. The beautiful part is that you get to create this identity through your actions, words, and mindset. I no longer identify myself as an athlete or salesman. I am a career driven entrepreneur, author, and businessman. What is your identity?

Learn to Sell Everything

Specialization over variety has always been a widely debated and researched topic across many different fields. Sports, music, dance, science—the list goes on. The dispute is centred on if it is more beneficial to specialize and focus on one specific parameter from the very beginning and not waiver from it, OR should an individual transition freely from one focus to another within a given field. The latter allows the learning of different skills, dealing with different obstacles, and rewiring one's brain for scenarios that cannot be replicated in a parallel field.

Having a very extensive background in sport (I know, sports again, but there is a good chance that others can relate to this in different ways as well), I was very drawn to this topic. I played every sport that I had time to attend. Football, hockey, baseball, soccer, basketball, volleyball. You name it, I played it. As I began working my way through the ranks of each sport, I slowly began to centralize my attention on a select few, before shedding all of them and focusing on just one- football. I look back and truly feel like it chose me, as it was originally not my primary sport of choice. However, through process of elimination, I found myself drawn to the sport and quickly accelerated in my progression when I realized it was something that I could pursue at a higher level.

When you consider that football was the last sport that I joined, and how it quickly became the sport I was best at, you can see the correlation from my own experience. Much in the same way that this situation would apply to musicians, doctors, and artists. They have access to a variety of different instruments, medical fields, and artistic designs before finding one that they gravitate to and specialize in. I truly feel this applies to salespeople as well.

The book 'Range' by David Epstein really dives into the debate of this. The research appears to support my feeling that you should learn to sell a variety of different products and services across a number of different industries. This will not only help better yourself as a salesperson and individual but will also broaden your self-awareness and show what you can accomplish. In my opinion, the biggest mistake one can make is selling a product solely based on the fact it was the first industry they were exposed to, especially if they are not feeling empowered and invested in what they are selling. It is okay to diverge from your current path to pursue a different avenue within sales. It is important to not feel like you are starting over again, and to understand that everything you learn along the way adds to your toolbox of knowledge. Your previous experience selling a widget will help you sell a gadget in another industry. Just because you pivot to something else does not start you back at square one; all of your experiences will lead you to greatness if you continue to commit yourself to your goals. If you do this—trust me—you will find your passion and you will create success.

The best personal example I can give to you is from a job I had working in sports hospitality. As I mentioned before, at the time, I believed this was the perfect opportunity for me. Given my background and the fact that I was drawn to sales, I thought it was an ideal match. I learned as much as I could and tried my best to be successful at the company, but it was a lost cause. I look back now and realize that my first instinct was to apply with one of the competitors within the same industry which is exactly what I did. I had heard about them while working with my original company and knew they operated within the same city. I applied, received the position, and found myself having more success with them; I had more freedom selling and was enjoying the office atmosphere. However, after 4-6 months, I was falling into the same patterns and finding myself in a rut. I realized that I was no longer drawn to the industry and the way it operated.

I spoke with people in the office who had been selling the hospitality for their entire lives and, not only did they not seem to be enjoying themselves, but they were also not experiencing an exponential amount of success over the others. There was no significant correlation between their results and their experience. At this point I realized two things:

1) I needed to cut ties with this industry
2) Experience within an industry does not always equal more success

Let me be clear on one thing before we move on from this topic—I am not saying that experience within an industry will not ultimately lead to more success. What I want to stress is that you should not be afraid to differentiate between industries throughout your career. Meet new people, learn new techniques, and remove yourself from your comfort zone. You will find that you're able to transition skills from every step of your career into your new endeavours. With a full toolbox, confidence, and the help of new mentors within the industry, you will find yourself excelling faster than you could have ever imagined.

PART V

HOW TO RE-MOTIVATE YOURSELF

S ALES IS A GRIND, PLAIN and simple. If you have reached this point of the book, then you know sales is not for the faint of heart. It's incredible how often I speak with people from outside the industry who believe sales is just an entry level job or only for people who could not cut it in a more advanced profession. These same people believe they could easily step into a sales role and have success. Maybe they have had poor experiences with cookie-cutter and manipulative salespeople or maybe they are just ignorant to have this projection upon people in the sales profession. I whole-heartedly disagree, and frankly, their opinion is of no concern to me.

Taking this into account, it is important to remember that the aforementioned grind can wear on you. Day after day, the stress of having to sell to provide a living for yourself can build and cause burn out. By this point, you already know my strong sentiment towards the importance of long-term motivation and why you need to have that beacon guiding you. However, from a day to day standpoint motivating yourself can be a little trickier. We all have stretches of bad days with the culminating risk of getting into a "rut". While this is normal, most salespeople don't get to rely on a steady paycheque just for showing up; we have to perform at our job on a consistent basis. This expedites the importance of getting ourselves back on track as quickly as possible.

I am going to break these up into intermediate and micro-solutions to help prevent these ruts and how to shake them if you're in one.

Intermediate

Monthly and weekly goals

This is the critical second step in the progression of our long-term goals that we already established previously in the book. We need to break these down into monthly and weekly activity objectives to ensure we stay the course. At the end of each month, take the time to review the goals that you set out in order to gauge what you were able to accomplish. These should not all be work specific and should mix in a number of categories to help prevent monotony. Examples can include: Physical, social, family, financial, and personal. The important factor remains that you are able to complete the tasks. The accountability built-up in these time frames is strengthening your habitual wiring and should create a sense of pride within yourself.

These monthly goals should be engineered in a way that is steering you towards your long-term goals. The splicing of your long-term goals provides landmarks that allow you to see your progress. As you become better at completing these tasks, continue to build upon these accomplishments, pushing yourself to achieve more within these specific time frames. One of the biggest risks of developing a rut is the feeling of a goal being too far in the distance. This will cause you to question if you will ever be able to accomplish it, and you could begin to second guess yourself. Monthly guidelines allow you to break these larger goals into digestible chunks and provides a more manageable game plan.

Furthermore, your weekly goals are a continued breakdown of your monthly goals. I personally feel that these provide a more tangible indicator of production to prevent those dangerous ruts from forming. I find a flexible weekly schedule far more effective than rigid, pre-planned daily activities. By having realistic weekly goals, it allows us to have those off days without creating a sense of internal guilt and a feeling of falling behind. A good example would be attempting to go on a diet by saying you want to lose 10lbs in a month. Without it being broken down into a weekly plan, you will most likely stray from your goal as there is no structure for what you need to do to achieve it.

Opposite to this, a strict daily routine causes feelings of failure if not adhered to perfectly. Day-to-day flexibility is important for unexpected nights out with friends that may include pizza and dessert or a stressful day with the kids and work. If you're confined to these strict daily guidelines, you will be overwhelmed by the feeling of failure and say to yourself that you might as well start again next week. The proper mentality would be to recognize that this was just an off-day and weekly objectives can still be met. Professional goals can work the exact same way. If you load up your daily agenda so heavily that tasks left unfinished feel like 10lbs anchors holding you back, the domino effect can cause stress and panic, and ultimately derail subsequent days. I call this "I'll start again Monday" syndrome. I have found the most effective way to navigate this is to form a daily checklist of important tasks you would like to accomplish that day.

This schedule is centred around absolutes like meetings, appointments, and mandatory timelines. From there, sprinkle in the tasks that further make up your weekly goals (exercising, prospecting, reading, yoga, social, etc.) that fit around your schedule. This reverts back to our previous point that some days are going to be different than others and you need to manage your efficiency accordingly. Not all days are going to be positive, energetic, and productive. However, as you create your next daily checklist, the activities that you were unable to complete the day before are still going to be listed and have not magically disappeared.

Tasks are going to continue to appear until they have been accomplished and crossed off. For example, if on Tuesday you planned to research new prospects but you found yourself tied up in an unexpected meeting, prospecting would not go to the wayside, it will be added back to the list the next day as you try to be more efficient on Wednesday. Also, by planning a week's worth of activities and goals ahead of time, you will already know which days are filled with absolutes, allowing you to pre-plan which days you must utilize more efficiently at the start of the week. You are now able to strategically plan your week without being disrupted by an off day. The effectiveness of physically writing it down reinforces the need to get this done within the timeline set. It's amazing how quickly a thought will be discarded when it is only recognized in passing, with no action taken to cement its importance.

The final step of this process is the continued review of these self-appointed goals at the end of each week and month to track how well you are holding yourself accountable. If you are completing your goals on a regular basis – great—keep going and continue to gradually increase them in scale. On the other hand, if you are having difficulties keeping these promises to yourself week-to-week (which will inevitably escalate month-to-month), then further reflection is immediately required. I understand that some goals may not always be met for any number of reasons; the major red flag presents itself with a consistent inability to reach your preplanned objectives.

"In self-trust all virtues are comprehended" was famously written by 19th century philosopher Ralph Waldo Emerson and I feel that this perfectly summarizes the importance of this section. If you realize that you are writing down arbitrary goals with no real importance placed on whether you accomplish them or not, they are not worth the paper you're writing them on. Accountability towards yourself is the underlying factor for success in your personal and professional life. Until this is truly achieved, this advice will have no merit. You must look in the mirror and tell yourself that you are prepared to follow

the guidelines that **you** are committing to. Otherwise, your goals will not be attained, and mediocrity will be a reoccurring theme in your life.

If you find yourself not finishing what you set out to accomplish and continue to encounter unmet goals, I encourage you to re-evaluate your long-term goals and determine if your foundational motivators are, in fact, as gravitational as you once thought. When these are harmonized with your deep personal beliefs, you will find yourself accomplishing weekly and monthly goals as intended.

Micro-Actions

Frustration and a rollercoaster of emotions within a 24-hour time span are a staple for any sales professional. Managing these emotions is important to keep yourself on track and preventing personal volatility throughout the day. You will be spoken to negatively and shown disrespect on some days, while on others you will lose sure-fire deals that you believed were all but signed. On the flip side, there will be days where you will have a spring in your step, customers will be reaching out to you, and you'll secure deals where all of your previous hard work culminated to the perfect close. Both will create extremely polarizing feelings that need to be handled accordingly to highlight the positives and curtail the lows.

In terms of the positives, review the entire sales cycle as it transpired and take written and mental notes. This reflection will allow you to recount what has worked for you in the past and incorporate these important factors into future encounters. Enjoy the feeling of success and allow it to continually drive you. I have also found it particularly important to come up with a personal reward system for your own hard work. It doesn't have to be extravagant in any way, and early on you definitely do not want to make this an expensive endeavour. However, make it something personal, enjoyable, and worthwhile. Sales is hard, and this should be gratifying to you. It is fun to associate something pleasurable with the act of achievement to keep you motivated.

Be sure to never lose the enjoyment of making a sale.

On the contrary, you will most likely be dealing with the negative side of this coin more often than not, especially early on. You know yourself better than I do, so I can only speak for myself, but you need to realize that it is not personal when a prospect lashes out. The longer you allow the negative thoughts to swirl in your head, the longer it takes you to centre yourself and get back to work. Recognize that if something minor has irked you, the easiest solution is to get right back at it and speak to the next prospect. This is the best way to put yourself in a new situation for a potentially positive encounter in order to help put an end to the previous experience.

It is important to clear your mind before the next phone call as you do not want to bring negativity into your next interaction. This can be easily detectable by prospects and can lead to a snowball effect of poor calls. If you find yourself in one of these spirals, or have a particularly negative conversation with a customer, it is best to quickly remove yourself from your environment before returning and continuing to work.

An easy solution to this is heading for a quick coffee, retreating to the break room for a few minutes, going for a walk, reviewing your weekly and monthly goals, or simply going over the situation with a manager or co-worker to vent and hear some reassuring words. Every workplace environment is structured differently, so you will have to find out what you will have access to in these times. The key is to set-up a game plan if you notice yourself being affected by how your day is progressing. Understand your workplace boundaries in the office, as you can't be heading to the break room after every bad call. Do your best to learn how you react to difficult interactions and respond accordingly as you develop a thicker skin and gain experience. These quick exercises should refocus your attention and actively realign you with your goals.

PART VI

WHERE TO GO FROM HERE

As I STATED AT THE beginning of the book, this is just the start. I cannot stress this enough! The situation that I have witnessed countless times is one where great salespeople with tremendous potential find themselves lost, trying to navigate through this profession on their own. They become discouraged, lose their motivation, and inevitably fade away into a different career path leaving behind opportunity, growth, freedom, and self-income. I say this with certainty because it almost happened to me. Thankfully, opportunity presented itself and gave me a second chance. I don't want you to fall victim to these same pitfalls that I and countless others have succumbed to. This does not mean that everyone reading this will have long prosperous sales careers. However, for some of you, I promise that if you heed this advice, it will be the first step in a journey that will lead to more wealth, prosperity, and personal growth than you could have ever imagine.

Become a Professional

You now have the building blocks to construct your foundation and the positive habits needed to focus your drive for success. It will take time to implement, practice, and gain experience with these basic first steps, but with time and patience, it will come. Once you have been able to achieve some consistency and belief, it will be time to truly become a professional in sales. This can mean different things to different people, but to me, it means you are committing to the concept that sales will be your career.

You are going to leverage your ability and successes in sales to build your wealth, support yourself and your family, and commit yourself to becoming the best possible salesperson you can be. The most important advice that I ever received and can pass along to you is that **you can never stop learning in sales**. You can never achieve perfection in sales. It would take ten lifetimes to soak in all of the information accessible to you in this profession and you can only continue to learn and digest knowledge and consistently chase a better version of yourself.

The best analogy I have ever read was from Zig Zigler who asked "would you ever seek medical advice or treatment from a doctor who had not picked up a book or attended a seminar since medical school?" Of course not. What kind of professional would not keep up with modern medical advice, research papers, and industry news. In sales, we are not dealing with life and death when it comes to our continued education, but we are dealing with our livelihood and the dependence of others, which may include your spouse, children, extended family or whatever situation you find yourself in. When we do not better our sales skills and fail to remain focused and motivated, we leave income, growth, and potential on the table and only hurt ourselves. If you're going to commit to this profession, go all in.

How to Go All in

Books/Audiobooks

The first is a no-brainer. The fact that you're reading or listening to this is proof that you are already on the right path to bettering yourself. There are so many amazing books written by incredible salespeople that will leave you more skilled, motivated, and further prepared than you could have ever anticipated. I have read countless books and listened to even more audiobooks that have left me inspired and made me an overall better sales professional.

The reason that I have gravitated towards audiobooks is that, being in outside sales, I have plenty of "windshield" time. I have learned to leverage my travel time with audiobooks. I found that I would finish one book every three months when reading, but that I could go through one per week when listening. A model that I have found extremely helpful is to listen to an audiobook once, and then immediately listen to it again at 1.25x the speed, as I find I retain much more the second time around (Assuming the book offers enough value to warrant a second listen). I recommend that you use this strategy if you have travel time, use public transit, or generally retain information better through listening.

Everyone is different, so use the best formula that suits your personal circumstances. Below, I have listed the books that have helped me the most. I encourage you to read/ listen to all of the ones on this list and the ones I mentioned throughout the book. I also challenge you to go out and explore new books that teach, inspire, and encourage you along your journey. Please email me or reach out on social media with any books that you recommend so that I can read them myself and help promote.

- *Never Split the Difference*—Chris Voss
- *Pitch Anything*—Oren Klaff
- *Flip the Script*—Oren Klaff
- *Atomic Habits*—James Clear
- *The Closers Survival Guide*—Grant Cardone
- *Be Obsessed or Be Average*—Grant Cardone
- *How to Become a Rainmaker*—Jeffery J. Fox
- *Little Red Book of Selling*—Jeffery Gitomer
- *New Sales Simplified*—Mark Weinberg
- *The Perfect Close*—James Muir
- *Secrets of Closing the Sale*—Zig Ziglar

Podcasts

The best part about podcasts is that they are ever evolving- they can be done daily, weekly, monthly, etc. How to find podcasts can vary, but normally they are sourced on: Apple Music, Spotify, Apple Podcast, Amazon Music, and more. There are plenty of great sales podcasts out there that cover plenty of topics that directly relate to the ebbs and flows that you will face on a daily basis. Even better, you can typically find podcasts tailored for your specific industry. This will allow you to really hone-in on specific market trends that relate to information you need to know on an ever-updating timeline. Again, not all podcasts will be helpful and the individuals hosting them will have a diverse range of knowledge and experience. Search around and see if you can find a few that you can really enjoy listening to. *I did not list any current ones as they may not be relevant or updated by the time you get to them.*

Blogs/Daily Emails

Blogs and podcasts are one and the same. Both can be updated regularly and contain extremely useful industry information and general sales knowledge. The most important part about blogs and podcasts that relate to you is that they are ever-expanding and stay relevant. Also, with blogs, information can be pulled from other locations that you may not be familiar with and reposted on the blog you follow. It's an ever-intertwining platform that helps connect you with leaders in your industry and gurus within the sales profession. The key is to find ones you enjoy and subscribe to them so that you are alerted or emailed every time a new post is released. Keep in mind, some blog sites become dormant and fail to provide further insight and information. Always be on the lookout for more if some of your favourites slow down with updates.

Daily emails are a great way to stay up to date on your industry, world news, or any other interests you have. Usually they are a quick 5-10min read to update you on events in a concise manner. It prevents you from having to use multiple sources every day and gets the juices flowing without cutting into your efficient morning routine. An example of one that I currently use is Morning Brew.

Seminars

Seminars are a great way to re-motivate yourself. As previously mentioned, one of the biggest things you'll find in sales is that it is a rollercoaster of emotions; and sometimes it can be mentally draining and you may need a reset. Other times, you will hear the same advice from the same people and need a fresh perspective from an outside source. It is important to stay organized and take notes because there is usually a lot of information being shared throughout a seminar covering a wide range of topics. It is also key to review your notes after the seminar so you can put together a game plan to implement new strategies to help grow your sales initiative. Not everyone has the luxury of living in a larger city that hosts a sales seminar or the budget to travel to one, and this is where resources like YouTube are helpful. There are plenty of great seminars recorded and uploaded to YouTube with extremely useful information. If you can watch one a month instead of watching a movie or a TV series, you will continue to put yourself ahead of the competition.

YouTube

YouTube has become an ever-growing source of information for sales representatives. Now that the monetary value of popular YouTube channels has been exposed, there is a large number of intelligent entrepreneurs providing a wealth of knowledge for free. Much like a blog or podcast these can be updated at a higher rate to stay relevant. Search through the videos and follow the content creators that you find enjoyable and applicable to your sales industry. The second benefit is that user often upload full seminars, Tedtalks, and conferences online. This allows you access to the same information that others travelled to and paid for, all at your fingertips.

Become the Extra Value

The most important thing that you can do when you become comfortable with your sales role is to begin separating yourself from the rest. This applies to all facets of the job. The harder you work and the more you apply yourself to your profession, the more success you will see. That is no secret. This is why I found my connection with sports to be such an asset when I entered sales.

If you don't allow yourself to be outworked by others, the results and recognition will follow. If you put in the extra work, you will begin to widen the gap between you and your colleagues, as well as your competition. Your customers will notice the extra effort you put in to keep them satisfied, and your managers will observe the improvements in your work and the sharpening of your skills. To be this extra value, you must be willing to put in the work away from the office, beyond your baseline expectations.

As I continue to reiterate, examples of this include: reading books before you go to bed, listening to audiobooks and podcasts during your commute to work, and browsing blogs and articles related to your industry in your free time.

Sales has never been and will never be a 9-5 job. If this is how you approach your career, you will struggle to keep your head above water and will never make enough of an impact to reap the rewards that obtained through hard work. If you continue to implement the building blocks provided and grow with the information supplied from external sources, you will become the extra value that separates you from the rest. These are the work habits that lead to promotions, raises, bonuses, commissions, and freedom without ever compromising your integrity. Becoming the extra value allows you to lead the pack and puts you in the driver seat of your career.

Develop Leadership

All Great Leaders are Sales Professionals

Whether it is selling a product, service, vision, or concept, all great leaders are masters at the sales profession. Researching for this book gave me the opportunity to really dive into how interconnected our work, social, and personal lives are linked. It is often stated but rarely analyzed that you are always "selling yourself". I believe it is far more present than we realize, especially at a subconscious level. Humans are constantly selling ideas, opinions, decisions, and their personal brand on a daily basis. These are the factors that shape our influence and ultimately showcase our character.

Because this is a regular occurrence, and one we are mostly unaware of, it can have both a positive and negative effect on those around us. A true double-edged sword. The more conscious you become of these interactions, the more you allow yourself to harness the power of the exchange. Being cognisant of this permits you to strengthen not only your work skills, but your personal life as well. Becoming a better spouse, parent, coach, and friend allows you to become better in your work environment, and ultimately, a superior individual to do business with.

Great leaders and sales professionals have always used this to their advantage while gaining influence and success. They understand that every conversation is an opportunity to showcase themselves and ensure that it is a positive interaction. It is extremely important to maintain integrity while presenting yourself and any influence gained should be used for the betterment of all parties. Always remember, your reputation precedes you. This especially rings true in sales. Be sure to reflect your true character. Dale Carnegie's book 'How to win friends and influence people' dives into more detail on this and is worth the read if you would like to learn more on this topic.

Realize that in the business world, every interaction is a sample of yourself and the value you bring to the situation. Whether it is with a co-worker, boss, manager, customer, or consultant. You are selling yourself and maneuvering your cog within the wheel. The sooner you understand this, the sooner you can utilize these relations to your advantage. I ask that you do not confuse this as manipulation, you are simply portraying your personal brand, work ethic, and knowledge with each interaction in a positive manner. As you continue to harness the power of positive interaction, as all great leaders do, you can now transition this influence and utilize it in your sales career. Over time, this will become second nature to you and become more natural. The more you understand the benefits you provide to customers, your company, and yourself the more you are able to 'sell' these qualities to others and harvest the benefits from it.

Become a Mentor

If you're reading this book in one shot, or have yet to implement some of these new habits and strategies, this will be more advanced than you currently need to be. However, I want you to keep this information on hand so that you can resort back to it when you're ready. Realize that you've jump-started your sales career by having a cheat sheet of proven positive habits to follow, and negative ones to break or avoid completely. If used correctly and implemented as soon as possible, you should excel past other individuals starting in this profession. With this, you will inevitably have people reaching out to you for advice, wondering how they can achieve similar results.

At the beginning of this book, I discussed the different types of people and personalities that you will meet in this profession and I urge you to take the right path and become a positive influence for others. I have witnessed far more positive, helpful, genuine people succeed in this industry than self-absorbed ones. This is no coincidence. For someone to have enough respect and admiration for you, to approach and ask for advice is something that should be looked at with pride and not taken for granted.

A mentor's role has so many benefits- not only are you helping out a fellow colleague or friend, but you're also giving yourself an opportunity to look at a new situation from an outsiders' perspective. This will allow you to give unbiased advice that best fits the circumstances while having their best interest in mind. This will only help you moving forward in your own career as you'll gain experience in this new situation or strengthen decision-making abilities in a scenario you may have struggled with in the past. Experience is the ultimate wisdom that can only be acquired by immersing yourself in the heat of the action and allowing yourself to learn from each challenge you're presented with. It is also a well-researched fact that the best way to learn something is to teach it; mentorship provides this opportunity.

Always try to remember the way that you felt when you first walked into the office and didn't know who to turn to when you needed advice or assistance. There are circumstances where new employees don't feel comfortable reviewing situations with a manager and need to look to their peers. Be that person that they can turn to; it will pay dividends for everyone involved.

Think Bigger

As I always preach to those who will listen, the best thing about sales is having the ability to create your own wealth and success. With this in mind, always think big when looking at your career goals. Understand that putting more time and effort into honing your craft and improving yourself in all capacities will incrementally add up and lead to a life you can now dream of and attain. There is a very high probability that the sales job you begin your career in will not be with the same company you end with. If it is, great! If not, that's normal.

My suggestion is to think big when changing companies or industries. As discussed, one of the biggest problems that plagued me early in my career was moving laterally within my industry to remain in my comfort zone even though I wasn't completely happy there. I hesitated to take risks which slowed my development as I wasn't learning new skills and advancing in sales. When I finally went for it in a completely new industry where I needed to start from scratch, I developed new techniques, pushed myself, renewed my sense of purpose in my career, and started to see my potential filter through.

I was given more responsibility and freedom to create my own sales process, and through trial and error, I was able to learn what worked and what didn't. I would not have had this freedom if I had not taken the time in the first few years of my career mastering the basics. Eventually, after you feel that you have put the time and sweat equity into a certain position, you can now think bigger and move up or move on.

If you enjoy being at your current company, your first option should be to request a promotion internally. It will show your commitment to them as an organization and to your own personal growth. If you feel you have shown your worth and outgrown your current role, a good organization will respect your request and either offer a new role or provide a clear and agreed upon game-plan to groom you for a position in the near future. If the company you are with is stalling your progression or the product/industry has lost its luster, do not be afraid to challenge your skills and bet on yourself. Look for a better salary and/or commission structure, look for a more flexible schedule, or try to sell something you're more passionate about. In sales, you are the only person who can hold you back, so don't get in your own way!

CONCLUSION

FIRST AND FOREMOST, I HOPE this has been as educational and informative for you to read as it has been for me to write. It's amazing how much self-reflection and nostalgia I went through in the process of outlining this book. Some of the memories, both good and bad, took me right back to moments that I remembered like they were yesterday. Things like my first training sessions, making my first sale, closing my biggest sales, and most importantly the people I have met along the way. Many of these people are incredibly genuine and I will be forever indebted to them for their help; most are still friends of mine to this day.

Even the bad memories of being cussed out, hung up on, and deals that fell through at the last minute can now bring a smile to my face. This helps give me perspective in the moment that even the worst situations pass, and hindsight will provide experience. As you venture into the profession of sales, I hope that you can adapt to the opportunities that are presented and navigate through the turbulence that you will inevitably encounter. Learn to enjoy the milestones in the moment and cherish the accomplishments you're able to attain. Allow the disappointment and turmoil to hurt, but don't allow it to dwell within and scar you. Strength from these moments will propel you further than any sale ever will.

I hope that you've been able to recognize that I did not write this book from a thousand-mile view. I have lived through the experiences I have written about, and the practices outlined are ones that I still hold myself accountable to daily. Even though some habits are easier than others to follow on a consistent basis, they all have their place in the process.

There is no surprise that when I resort back to the basics, I find success no matter what my career has thrown at me. In difficult times or when going through a dry spell, I have often referred back to these fundamentals to help myself out. I hope you are able to do the same. This book is meant to provide the foundation of basic fundamentals that need to be practiced on a daily basis. When you find yourself in trying times, take a moment to reflect and see if you are following the basic principles. If not, pull this book off the shelf to remind yourself of the actions that helped get you to where you are today. Even though we are constantly socializing in this profession, it can be a lonely and isolated place when things are not going our way. Sometimes you must go all the way back to the beginning to realign yourself.

My final hope is that you find joy and prosperity in the career of professional sales. It truly is a gratifying profession that eventually gives back what you put into it. Although it may seem cruelly inconsistent during the infancy stages of your career, the more you continue to reinvest in yourself through all of the platforms listed earlier in the book the sooner you will be able to reap what you sew. It is important in these moments not to ease up as you begin to find success.

"*Things may come to those who wait, but only the things left by those who hustled.*" Although the source of this quote is debated, I believe it brilliantly describes the mentality you need to have in sales. You can never truly take your foot off the pedal as you gain momentum. Complacency should never follow your triumph. I understand that as you grow, more important influences will enter your life in the form of family and commitments; this is why it is critical to continually rewrite your goals and determine your fundamental motivation. What you are able to accomplish in your sales career will directly influence the experiences you will be able to share with your family, and give you the financial freedom to enjoys these moments. These habits will help you to utilize your time efficiently when it comes to balancing your work and personal life. The efforts you put in now will continue to grow exponentially like compound interest in a financial portfolio.

I appreciate you joining me on this journey to learn the ropes as a beginner in sales. Keep this book close for reference at any time, and always remind yourself of the basics when you become overwhelmed; there will be ups and downs no matter how much experience you gain. It is important to refer to your long and short-term goals to help provide balance without overwhelming yourself in any one moment. Challenge yourself, embrace a changing environment, and learn to adapt to new situations.

Understand that no two sales will be identical, but the overlapping similarities will allow you to recognize the parallels and this experience will help guide you. Most importantly, if you take the time to learn and grow within your profession, there truly are no limits in sales. There is no shortage of material to help you and cultivate your potential. Be sure to use every resource at your disposal because, at the end of the day, as Warren Buffett has always said "*The most important investment you can make is in yourself.*"

Learn to better yourself in all facets of life, not just sales, and you will see the rewarding connection between the habits of personal growth and the enjoyment of continued success. Even though there is no finish line in the career of sales, there are milestones. I hope this book has provided you with enough knowledge to reach your first. I leave the rest in your capable hands as we continue to pursue our goals together. I wish you all the best in your sales career!

> ** Feel free to reach out to me throughout your journey on any number of different social media platforms to share your questions, career decisions, dilemmas, and of course success stories. **

POST-SCRIPT REFLECTION

FULL TRANSPARENCY, THIS PROJECT TOOK far longer than expected to complete. Not necessarily because of the material, although early-on, I re-wrote many of the subjects contained in the book before I felt confident enough that the information conveyed was to its highest quality. It had to do with an internal struggle believing that I could truly help those starting in the sales profession. I had plenty of material already written, but the belief in my message would sway, and when it did, I would put off the next steps in writing to the bottom of my to-do list and go back to focusing on my own career.

It wasn't until the world was brought to a standstill by the 2020 global pandemic that my to-do list suddenly became vacant. The constant distractions that kept me from facing my fears with this book became obsolete and I met a proverbial fork in the road. I either confronted what was preventing me from finishing or throw away the idea of writing this book entirely. Although the notion of the latter crossed my mind, I knew this would lead to a domino effect, impacting my personal beliefs toward my own abilities and carrying out goals that I felt certain I would achieve. Ultimately, I used this additional time to not only re-word and tinker many of my prior topics, but also develop and expand on new ones that I had not previously thought to add. After countless late nights of writing and critiquing I felt more excited than ever about the material I had amassed, even though I was far from a completed product.

Then a funny thing happened, something I had not expected. As I began to piece together sections of the book into a format that I felt created flow and linear importance to the reader, it was finally time for me to read the rough draft in full, for the first time. Although it was still riddled with spelling errors, grammatical mistakes, and run-on sentences, the overall message of the book, more than ever, became clear. The puzzle pieces began to connect stronger than I had ever imagined. As I moved towards the latter half of the book, the self-reflection began to emerge; I was unable to progress more than a page or two without pondering if I was straying from my core values and self-motivations. Converting from the writer to the reader was far more powerful than I could have ever expected. Was I starting to resist change and sacrificing my own beliefs for my job? Did I still believe in everything I was representing at my company? Was I restricting my growth opportunity by denying myself a career change? It is safe to say, self-reflection and time have a powerful way of piercing suppressed personal thoughts.

After I completed reading the first draft of the book and began the long, arduous, editing process, I couldn't help but to consider if I was leading by example with the words I was writing. It was eating away at me. Integrity and transparency are extremely important to me in both personal life and career. I believe it is a core value in becoming a proficient professional in sales. With that in mind, I re-read this book again and took a leap of faith. I revamped my resume and sought out to find a career more in-line with my values while also offering growth opportunity and long-term sustainability.

My former company (the one I was employed at while writing most of this book) provided me an opportunity for which I will be forever grateful. They allowed me the freedom to create my own sales formula and run my territory as I saw fit. This was a luxury that I previously, had not been granted. I was able to learn from my mistakes and continually evolve a structure where I was able to be genuine and ultimately create relationships by being myself. It showed me the true benefit of growing a territory based on relationships and long-term success and not "one and done" sales.

The path to long-term success in your career is built on the foundation of current actions. There were highs and lows along the way, but six years later, I am a better person and a much better sales professional than I was when I started. However, over time, gaps and discrepancies began to show between my own beliefs and the ones presented by others. Personal support seemed limited within the company, and I felt a culture shift. In the end, I felt a transformation was needed from a personal and professional stand point.

For the first time in a long time, my life was beginning to show uncertainty for me. We were all still in a pandemic and I was looking to shift careers in an unpredictable world. So, what did I do? I decided to become my own case study. I chose to follow all of the advice that I advocated in this book. I made drastic changes to my resume and updated it to corollate with the current hiring market, formulated personal cover letters, and researched companies before interviews. I did not limit my applications to companies within the same industry and tried to find companies that were renown for offering the best value in their market.

It was a long process, especially with everything being done virtually. However, after the dust has settled, I feel happier and more confident in my choice than I could have ever imagined. I ended up in a whole new industry, new product, new compensation structure, and new growth opportunities. I also found a company culture that is second to none; one that inspires their employees and look to develop from within. They empower their people to be better and reward them for their business accomplishments as well as their teamwork and coaching. What comes next is still left to be found out, but I feel more comfortable than ever in saying that change is not something that should be feared, but instead embraced. Trust in your own abilities and beliefs and you will find success.

The point of this is not to say when things start to waiver, abandon ship and find something new. However, there comes a point when you recognize these changes do not align with your personal beliefs and its okay to make adjustments in order to manage your own well-being. It is challenging and scary expanding beyond your comfort zone, but the rewards of doing so outweigh the regret of stagnancy.

I can say now with the utmost confidence that a sales career can provide your life with anything that you can imagine, but it must be earned. You have to be willing to lead your own journey through growth, education, adaptation, and desire. You will get what you put into it; the next chapter of your life is in your hands!

NOW THAT YOU HAVE COMPLETED the first and most important step in establishing yourself as a true sales professional, it's time to build on your momentum. The real fun is just beginning, and I would love to continue to be a part of your journey.

I encourage you to join our online community at **pitchingsalesconsulting.com** for free access to features like:

- ► Newsletters, blogs, and podcasts with insightful information that pertains to the sales profession;

- ► Helpful PDFs, charts, and important industry data;

- ► Links to my social media pages;

- ► Personal consultations options;

- ► Consistently updated book recommendations; and

- ► Community building: A way to reach out to me directly with your personal challenges, successes, book recommendations, goals, or any other thoughts and suggestions you wish to share.

Don't ever feel like you are on this journey alone. Join the community today!

www.ingramcontent.com/pod-product-compliance
Lightning Source LLC
Chambersburg PA
CBHW071432210326
41597CB00020B/3759